THE ROAD TO
SAN GIOVANNI

BOOKS BY ITALO CALVINO

THE
ROAD TO
SAN GIOVANNI

Italo Calvino

TRANSLATED FROM THE ITALIAN
BY TIM PARKS

Mariner Books
Houghton Mifflin Harcourt
BOSTON · NEW YORK

For information about permission to reproduce selections from this book,
write to Permissions, Houghton Mifflin Harcourt Publishing Company,
215 Park Avenue South, New York, New York 10003.

www.hmhco.com

First published in Italy as *La Strada di San Giovanni*
by Arnoldo Mondadori Editore, 1990

This translation first published in hardcover by Pantheon Books,
a division of Penguin Random House, in 1993,
and subsequently in paperback by Vintage Books, a division of
Penguin Random House, in 1994.

Library of Congress Cataloging-in-Publication Data is available.
ISBN 978-0-544-14652-5

Printed in the United States of America
DOC 10 9 8 7 6 5 4 3 2 1

CONTENTS

One day in the spring of 1985, Calvino told me he was going to write twelve more books. "What am I saying?" he added. "Maybe fifteen."

Doubtless the first was to be *Six Memos for the Next Millennium*. As far as the second and third were concerned, I think he had only a vague idea himself. He would write lists upon lists, changing some titles, altering the chronology of others.

Of the works he was planning, one was to be made up of a series of "memory exercises." I have brought together five of these here, written between 1962 and 1977. But I know he meant to write others: "Instructions for the Other Self", "Cuba", "The Objects". Hence I felt I couldn't use his working title, "Passaggi obbligati", since it seems that many of the passages are missing.

ESTHER CALVINO

PASSAGGI OBBLIGATI

- La strada di San Giovanni
- Autobiografia d'uno spettatore
- Ricordo di una battaglia
- La ~~giudici~~ 20 di...
- Cuba
- La poubelle agréée

  ~~...mi il...~~

  ~~Il debito...~~

  Gli spett...

THE ROAD TO
SAN GIOVANNI

A general explanation of the world and of history must first of all take into account the way our house was situated, in an area once known as "French Point", on the last slopes at the foot of San Pietro hill, as though at the border between two continents. Below, just beyond our gate and the private drive, lay the town with its pavements shopwindows cinema-posters newspaper-kiosks, then Piazza Colombo a few moments' walk away, then the seafront; above, you only had to go out of the kitchen door to the *beudo* that ran behind the house (you know what a *beudo* is, a ditch with a wall above and a narrow paving of flagstones beside running horizontally across the hill to take water from the streams to the fields) and immediately you were in the country, striking up cobbled mule tracks, between drystone walls and vineyard supports and greenery. That was the way my father always left the house, in his huntsman's clothes, with his leggins, and you could hear the step of his hobnail boots on the flags by the ditch, and the brass tinkle of his dog, and the squeak of the little gate that opened into the road that led to San Pietro. The way my father saw things, it was from here up that the world began, while the other part of the world below the house was a mere appendix, necessary sometimes when there were things to be done, but alien and insignificant, to be crossed in great strides, as though in flight, without looking to right or left. But I didn't agree, in fact quite the opposite: as I saw it, the world, the map of the planet, began on the other side of our house and went downwards, everything else being a blank space, with no marks and no meaning; it was down in the town that the signs of the future were to be read, from those streets, those nighttime lights that were not just the streets and lights of our small secluded town, but *the* town, a glimpse of all possible towns, as its harbour likewise was all the harbours of all the continents, and as I leaned out from the balustrades around our garden everything that attracted and bewildered me was within reach – yet immensely far away – everything was implicit, as the nut in its husk, the future and the present, and the harbour – still leaning out over those balustrades, and I'm not really sure if I'm talking about an age when I never left the garden or of an age when I would always be running off out and about, because now the two ages have fused together, and this age is one and the same thing as those places, which are no longer places nor anything else – the harbour, I was saying, you couldn't see, it was hidden behind the rooftops of the tall houses in Piazza Sardi and Piazza Bresca, only the strip of the wharf rising above them and the tips of the boats' masts; and the streets were hidden too and I could never get their layout to match that of the roofs, so unrecognizable did proportions and perspectives seem to me from up above: there the bell tower of San Siro, the pyramidal cupola of the Prince Amadeus Municipal Theatre, here the iron tower of the old Gazzano elevator factory (now that these things have gone forever, their names impose themselves on the page, irreplaceable

and peremptory, demanding salvation), the
mansards of the so-called Parisian Building, a
block of rented flats owned by cousins of ours,
which at that time (I'm talking about the late
twenties now) was an isolated outpost of distant
metropolises stranded on the rocky San Fran-
cesco River valley . . . Beyond all this, like a
curtain, the Porta Candelieri side of the river –
the water itself was hidden down at the bottom
with its reeds, its washerwomen, its scum of
refuse under the Roglio bridge – rose in a steep
hill where my family then owned a precipitously
sloping allotment, and where the old Pigna casbah clung on, grey and porous as a disinterred
bone, with bits that were tarry black or yellow
and tufts of grass, and above, on the site of the
old San Costanzo quarter, destroyed by the
earthquake of '87, was a public garden, neatly
kept and a little sad, whose hedges and espaliers
climbed up the hill: as far as the dancefloor of
a workingmen's club mounted on scaffolding,
the shabby building of the old hospital, the
eighteenth-century sanctuary of the Madonna
della Costa, with its imposing mass of blue.
Mothers' shouts, the songs of girls or of drun-
kards, depending on the time of day, on the day
of the week, would shear off from these super-
urban slopes to tumble down onto our garden,
clear through a sky of silence; while shut in

amongst the red scales of its roofs the city sounded its confused clatter of trams and hammers, and the lone trumpet in the courtyard of the De Sonnaz barracks, and the hum of the Bestagno sawmill, and – at Christmastime – the music of merry-go-rounds along the seafront. Every sound, every shape, led one back to others, more sensed than heard or seen, and so on and on.

My father's road likewise led far away. The only things he saw in the world were plants and whatever had to do with plants, and he would say all their names out loud, in the absurd Latin botanists use, and where they came from – all his life he'd had a passion for studying and acclimatizing exotic plants – and their popular names, too, if they had them, in Spanish or in English or in our local dialect, and into this naming of plants he would put all his passion for exploring a universe without end, for venturing time and again to the furthest frontiers of a vegetable genealogy, opening up from every branch or leaf or nervation as it were a waterway for himself, within the sap, within the network that covers the green earth. And in growing his plants – because that was another of his passions, or rather his main passion – in farming our San Giovanni estate (he would go there every morning leaving by the *beudo* door with his dog, half an hour's walk even at his pace, almost all of it uphill) he would be forever anxious, but as though it wasn't so much his getting a good yield out of those few hectares that he really cared about, as his doing whatever he could to further a task of nature which required human assistance, to grow everything that could be grown, to offer oneself as a link in a story that goes on and on, from the seed and the cutting for planting out or for grafting to the flower to the fruit to the plant and then over and over again without beginning or end in the narrow confines of the earth (the plot or the planet). But just a rustle of grass from beyond the strips of land he worked, a flutter, a squeak, and he would jump up eyes round and staring small beard pointed, to stand there ears straining (he had a motionless face, like an owl's, with sudden starts sometimes, like a bird of prey, eagle or condor), and he was no longer the farmer but the woodsman now, the hunter, because this was his passion – his first, yes, his first, or rather his last, the final shape of his one passion, to know to grow to hunt, in every way to get on top of things, inside them, in that wild wood, in the non-anthropomorphic universe, before which (and only there) a man was man – to hunt, to lie in ambush, in the cold night before dawn, on the bleak heights of the

Colla Bella or the Colla Ardente, waiting for the thrush, the hare (a pelt hunter, like all Ligurian farmers, his dog was a bloodhound) or to go right into the wood, to beat it inch by inch, dog's nose in the ground, for all the animal trails, in every gorge where over the last fifty years foxes and badgers had dug their lairs and only he knew where, or when he went without his gun – to the sort of place where thrusting mushrooms swell the sodden earth after rain or edible snails streak it, the familiar wood with its toponymy that went back to the time of Napoleon – Monsù Marco, the Corporal's Sash, Artillery Way – and every gamebird and every scent was reason enough to walk for miles off the paths, beating the mountainside gulley after gulley for days and nights, sleeping in those crude huts for drying chestnuts made from stones and branches that people call *cannicci*, alone with his dog or his gun, as far as Piedmont, as far as France, without ever leaving the woods, forcing open the path before him, that secret path that only he knew and that went across all the woods there were, that united all woods in one single wood, every wood in the world in a wood beyond all woods, every place in the world in a place beyond all places.

You see how our roads diverged, my father's and my own. Though I was like him in a way.

For what was the road I sought if not a repeat of my father's, but dug out of the depths of another otherness, the upperworld (or hell) of humanity, what were my eyes seeking in the dimly lit porches of the night (sometimes the shadow of a woman would disappear inside) if not the half-open door, the cinema screen to pass through, the page to turn that leads into a world where all words and shapes become real, present, my own experience, no longer the echo of an echo of an echo.

Talking to each other was difficult. Both verbose by nature, possessed of an ocean of words, in each other's presence we became mute, would walk in silence side by side along the road to San Giovanni. To my father's mind, words must serve as confirmations of things, and as signs of possession; to mine they were foretastes of things barely glimpsed, not possessed, presumed. My father's vocabulary welled outward into the interminable catalogue of the genuses, species and varieties of the vegetable world – every name was a distinction plucked from the dense compactness of the forest in the belief that one had thus enlarged man's dominion – and into technical terminology, where the exactness of the word goes hand in hand with the studied exactness of the operation, the gesture. And this whole Babel-like nomenclature was mashed up in an equally Babel-like idiomatic base, where various languages vied with each other, combining together as need or memory dictated (dialect for anything local and blunt – he had an unusually rich dialect vocabulary, full of words no one used anymore – Spanish for things general and decorous – Mexico had been the backdrop to his most successful years – Italian for rhetoric – he was, in everything, a nineteenth-century man – English – he had been to Texas – for the practical side, French for jokes), the result being a conversational style all woven together with stock refrains promptly trotted out in response to familiar situations, exorcizing the movements of the mind and forming once again a catalogue, parallel to that of his farming vocabulary – and to yet another catalogue of his made up not of words this time but of whistles, twitters, trills, tu-whits and tu-whoos, this arising from his great ability to mimic birdcalls, whether simply by pursing his lips or cupping his hands round his mouth in some particular way, or by using little whistles or gadgets that you blew into or that went off with a spring, a considerable assortment of which he would carry around with him in his hunting jacket.

I could recognize not a single plant or bird.

The world of things was mute for me. The words that flowed and flowed inside my head weren't anchored to objects, but to emotions fantasies, forebodings. And all it took was for a scrap of trampled newspaper to find its way beneath my feet and I would be engrossed in soaking up the writing on it, mutilated and un-mentionable – names of theatres, actresses, vanities – and already my mind would be racing off, the sequence of images would go on for hours and hours as I walked silently behind my father, who might point to some leaves on the other side of a wall and say, "Ypotoglaxia jas-minifolia" (I'm inventing the names; I never learned the real ones), "Photophila wolfoides", he would say (I'm inventing; they were names of this sort), or "Crotodendron indica", (of course I could perfectly well have looked up some real names, instead of inventing them, and maybe rediscovered what plants my father had actually been naming for me; but that would have been cheating, refusing to accept the loss that I inflicted on myself, the thousands of losses we inflict on ourselves and for which there is no making amends). (And yet, and yet, if I had written some real names of plants here it would have been a gesture of modesty and devotion on my part, finally resorting to that humble knowledge that my youth rejected in order to try my luck with other cards, unknown and treacherous, it would have been a way of making peace with my father, a demonstration of maturity, and yet I didn't do it, I indulged in this joke of invented names, this intended parody, sure sign that I am still resisting, arguing, sure sign that that morning march to San Giovanni is still going on, with its same discord, and that every morning of my life is still the morning when it's my turn to go with Father to San Giovanni.)

We had to go with my father to San Giovanni, one day me and one day my brother (not during school time, because then Mother wouldn't allow us to be distracted, but in the summer months, just when we could have slept late), to help him carry home the baskets of fruit and greens. (I'm talking about when we were bigger now, teenagers, and Father old; though Father always seemed to be the same age, between sixty and seventy, a dogged, tireless old age.) Summer and winter, he would get up at five, noisily pull on his farming clothes, lace up his leggins (he always dressed heavily, jacket and waistcoat whatever the season, mainly because he needed so many pockets for all the pruning shears and grafting knives and balls of string or raffia he always took with him; except that in summer he'd change his fustian hunting jacket and

peaked-cap-with-attached-balaclava for faded
yellow cloth fatigues left over from Mexico days
and a colonial lion-hunter's hat), come into our
room to wake us up, with gruff shouts and
shoulder-shaking, then go downstairs with his
hobnail shoes on the marble steps, wander
round the empty house (Mother got up at six,
then Grandmother, and last of all the maid and
the cook), open the kitchen windows, heat up
some coffee for himself, slops for the dog, talk
to the dog, get together the baskets to be taken
to San Giovanni, empty or with bags of seeds
or insecticide or fertilizer in them (the noises
sounded muffled to us in our semiconscious
state, since no sooner had Father woken us up
than we had fallen right back to sleep again),
and already he would be opening the back door
to the *beudo*, was out in the street, coughing
and clearing his catarrh, summer and winter.

We had managed to extract a tacit reprieve
from our morning duty: instead of walking along
with Father we would catch up with him in
San Giovanni, half an hour or an hour later, so
that his footsteps marching away up San Pietro
hill told us we still had a scrap of sleep to cling
to. But immediately my mother came to wake
us up again. "Get up, get up, it's late, Dad went
ages ago!" and she would open the windows onto
palm trees rustling in the morning wind, pull

the bedclothes off us, "Get up, get up, Dad's waiting for you to carry the baskets!" (No, it's not so much Mother's voice that comes back to me, in these pages echoing with my father's noisy and distant presence, but a silent authority she had: she looks out between these lines, then immediately withdraws, is left in the margin; there, she came into our room and is gone, we didn't hear her leave and our sleep is over forever.) I must get dressed in a hurry, climb up to San Giovanni before my father starts back, laden.

He always came back laden. It was a point of honour for him never to make the trip empty-handed. And since the proper road didn't go up as far as San Giovanni, there was no other way of getting the produce home than to carry it by hand (our hands, that is, since a labourer's time costs money and can't be thrown away, and when the women go to market they are already loaded up with things to sell). (True, there had once been – but this is a memory from earlier infancy – Giuà the muleteer with his wife Bianca and mule Bianchina, but Bianchina the mule had been dead a long time, and Giuà had got a hernia, though old Bianca is still alive today as I write.) Usually it was towards half-past nine or ten that my father got back from his morning trip: you would hear his footsteps along the *beudo*, heavier than when he set out, a bang on the kitchen door (he didn't ring the bell because he had his hands full, or perhaps more out of a kind of declaration, of emphasis of his coming back laden), and you would see him come in with a basket under each arm, or a hamper, and a haversack on his back or even a pannier, and the kitchen would suddenly be swimming in greens and fruit, there was always more than one family could eat (I'm talking here about the times of plenty, before the war, before tending the land became almost the only means of getting the food we needed), and my mother would disapprove, worried as ever that nothing should be wasted, things, time, energy.

(That life is partly waste was something my mother would not accept: I mean that it is partly passion. Hence she never left the garden where every plant was labelled, the house swathed in bougainvillea, the study with its herbariums and the microscope undere the glass dome. Always sure of herself, methodical, she transformed passions into duties and lived on those. But what pushed my father up the road to San Giovanni every morning – and me downwards along my own road – was not so much the duty of the hardworking landowner, the altruism of the agricultural innovator – and in my case not so much those definitions of duty that I would gradually impose on myself – but passion, fierce passion, pain of existence – what else could have forced him to scramble up through woods and wilderness and me to plunge into a labyrinth of walls and printed paper? – desperate confrontation with that which lies outside of ourselves, waste of self set against the waste of the world in general.)

My father never attempted to save energy, only time: he wouldn't shirk the steeper slope if it was the shorter. Depending on what stretches of mule track you chose, what short-cuts and bridges, there were all kinds of ways of getting from our house to San Giovanni: the route my father took was doubtless the result of long experience and numerous improvements and second thoughts; but by now it had become like the stairs at home, a series of steps you could climb with your eyes closed, taking up barely an instant of mental space, as if impatience had abolished both distance and effort. He only had to think: "Now I'll go to San Giovanni" (he'd suddenly remembered that a strip of Jerusalem artichokes hadn't been watered, that some aubergine seeds should be sprouting their first leaves) and it was as if he'd already been transported there, already he was seething inside with the scolding he was planning to give his workers or day labourers and the words would be bursting from his breast in an avalanche of insults for men and women alike, insults whose obscenity had lost all the warmth of complicity to become as austere and compact as a stone wall. This impatience, this intolerance at finding himself anywhere but on his own land, would sometimes seize him halfway through the day, when he'd already got back from his regular morning inspection at San Giovanni and changed into his town clothes, his starched collar, the waistcoat with the silver chain, a red fez he had bought in Tripolitania and wore in the house and the office to cover his bald head, and all of a sudden, in the middle of doing something else, he would think – because it was the estate that was always on his mind – of some job that hadn't been finished up at San Giovanni or that hadn't been done properly or of some worker who for lack of instructions might be standing idle, and immediately we would see him get up from his desk, go upstairs to his room, come down all togged up from hunting hat to leggins, untie the dog and go out by the door to the *beudo*, even in the hottest moments of a summer afternoon, staring straight ahead of him, the sun beating down.

From the *beudo* you went out onto the brick and cobbled steps of Salita San Pietro. Here you would meet old folks from the Giovanni Marsaglia Home in their grey caps with red initials (including, as everybody knew, Russian princes fallen upon hard times, lords who had gambled away fortunes on the Riviera) and nuns leading lines of little girls from the holiday camps for the Milanese and people climbing up to visit sick relatives in the New Hospital. The housing in this area – there was a stretch of paved road now – was the result of various stages of sedimentation: like everywhere else the place had once been a stretch of fields watched over by farmhouses; then at the turn of the century a few expensive villas had sprung up, their gardens waving with palms, like the house we lived in (my parents' first purchase on their return from America) and another a little further up the hill, built Indian style, all spindly steeples and domes, called "Palais d'Agra" (a name I always found mysterious until I read Kipling's *Kim*), and yet another converted into a municipal quarantine station, its shutters always closed; later on, the wealthy residential districts of the town moved elsewhere and the area was taken over by more modest little houses, homely cottages wth small pieces of land used for seedbeds and sheds for chickens or rabbits. So that as far as the Baragallo bridge you were walking through a district that was half rural but already under fierce attack from the town, the remains of the traditional agricultural life (an old olive mill where water and moss roared on rusted wheels; a winery, stained purple, with vats and presses) rubbing shoulders with garages, flower wholesalers, sawmills, brick storage yards, an electric-power plant full of windows that loomed bright empty and humming in the mornings before dawn, and beyond all these the huge rectangle of the housing project, first and only completed lot of a planned village, an "achievement of the Regime" begun with enthusiasm and left without sequel, but sufficing to remind you that this was already the Europe of the masses.

At the Baragallo bridge we would leave the road, which went on towards Madonna della Costa (we only walked that way when we went to see Uncle Quirino, nicknamed Titin, in the Calvinos' eighteenth-century house, its old pink stucco rising from a grey cloud of olive trees on top of the hill where my great-grandparents had once had their brick kilns), and follow the river. Immediately something changed, and the first sign of it was this: that as far as Baragallo, people, like people on suburban streets anywhere, didn't so much as look at one another, whereas after Baragallo everybody greeted everybody else as they passed by, even people they didn't know, with a loud "Mornin'," or

some other generic expression indicating rec-
ognition of the existence of their fellow man,
like: "Keep it up, keep it up," or "Aren't we
carrying a lot today," or a comment on the
weather, "Looks like rain to me," messages of
consideration and friendship full of discretion,
spoken as they went along, without stopping,
almost to themselves, barely raising their eyes.
My father too would change after Baragallo;
that nervous impatience that had marked his
step so far would disappear, likewise his irri-
tation when he shouted at the dog or tugged on
the leash; now he would look around more
calmly, the dog would usually be let loose and
the shouts and whistles and fingersnapping directed its way were more good-natured, even
affectionate. This feeling of being back in more
isolated, familiar places had its effect on me too,
but at the same time I would also feel uneasy
at no longer being able to think of myself as the
anonymous passerby of the street; from now on
I was "one of the professor's boys," subjected
to the scrutiny of every eye.

On the other side of a wooden fence pigs
shrieked and fought with each other (an unusual sight in our part of the world), bred by a
Piedmontese family who had set up the kind of
dairy farm typical of their home country. (On
the way up we would already have passed by

old Spirito driving his cart loaded with milk churns for his customers.) Opposite the pig farm the road gave onto a rocky stream, and there would be a row of women leaning over a sort of long raised trough washing clothes. Further on you could choose between two different paths, depending on whether or not you went back across the river over an ancient hump-backed bridge. If you didn't go over the bridge you followed some ditches and shortcuts running beside strips of farmland until you reached the San Giovanni mule track via a flight of recently built (or restored) steps which climbed so sharp and steep in bright sunlight it took your breath away. (After the last war, someone wrote an obscenity in huge tarred letters on a wall at the top of the steps, in mockery of those climbing up carrying things, perhaps to re-awaken an instinct of rebellion, or just seeking confirmation of his own hopelessness.) Then the mule track pushed on toward San Giovanni on the flat for a good while; the sea was behind us; on the other side of the river, the Tasciaire bank was slashed by a huge long gorge, testimony to an old landslide, a splash of blue in the splintered, earth-coloured stone. After rounding one particular bend you'd be able to see the little valley of San Giovanni opening up obliquely from the end of the main valley and so sharply lit that you could make out each separate strip of land and –where the olives didn't cloud your view – who was working there, and the smoke from the red roofs of the barns.

We liked to use this route going down; climbing up we found the other more attractive: having crossed the bridge, you climbed the hill along the Tasciaire mule track, likewise steep and exposed to the sun, but twisting and varied and paved with old, crooked, worn-out stones, so that it seemed painless and homely by comparison. Then you left the track to follow a long *beudo* which ran across the side of the valley halfway up, just below that huge gorge you could see from the other side. The *beudo* was raised over the farmed strips and you had to watch your step so as not to slip and sometimes you had to hang on to the crooked, bulging wall beside. The dog usually found that the safest way to go was in the ditch, padding along in the water. Here and there fig trees rose from the strips on either side and a green shadow shaded the *beudo*; some farmhouses had been built right up against it and walking along you could almost be inside them, mixed up in the lives of those families, all out at work since dawn, women and men and children digging the earth of their strip with dull blows from their *magaiu* (a three-pronged fork), or, using their *magaiu* again to "turn in the water", which meant knocking down the earth bank of the ditch and building other banks to lead the water twisting and turning through the seedbeds.

Further on, the *beudo* disappeared into a dense thicket of rustling reeds, and we had reached the river. This had to be forded with a zigzag of jumps across white stepping-stones following a pattern we knew by heart but which could always change when rainy days swelled the river and carried off one of the stones. Climbing up away from the river you cut across between the strips along private paths till you reached a shortcut that was itself half a stream, and as with the other path you now joined the San Giovanni mule track, but at a point much further on.

The nearer we got to San Giovanni, the more my father would be overcome by a new tension, which wasn't just a last burst of impatience to arrive at the only place he felt was his own, but also a sort of remorse at having been away for so long, his conviction that something must have been lost or have gone wrong during his absence, his urgency to cancel out everything in his life that was not San Giovanni, and at the same time a feeling that since San Giovanni was not the whole world but merely a corner of the world besieged by the rest, it would always spell despair for him.

But all it took was for someone at the top of a strip, pruning or spreading sulphate on the vines, to call down, "*Professore*, if you please, could I ask you a question?" and go on to ask advice about mixtures of fertilizers, the best time to make graftings, or about insecticides or the new seeds the Farming Consortium had in, and my father would stop and, cheering up, relaxing, exclamatory, a bit long-winded, explain the whys and wherefores. In short, all he wanted was a sign that civil cohabitation was possible in this world of his, a cohabitation prompted by a passion for improvement and informed by natural reason; but then he would immediately be oppressed again by reminders that all was precarious and beset by danger and once more the fury was upon him. And one of these reminders was myself, the fact that I belonged to that other, metropolitan and hostile part of the world, the painful awareness that he couldn't count on his children to consolidate this ideal San Giovanni civilization of his, which thus had no future. So that the last stretch of the path was covered in an unwarranted hurry, as though it were the edge of a blanket he could use to tuck himself away inside San Giovanni; and hurrying along like this we went by a decrepit olive mill inhabited by two even more decrepit old women, over the concrete bridge that went back across the river (the track began to climb a little again here), past Regin's house – he was a relative of ours and a customs officer whose dog would resume an interminable quarrel with our own, barking and leaping up (the track became steep here) – through the field of another relative, Bartumelìn, who had spent his youth in Peru (his wife, who we saw rinsing clothes in the washing trough, was a Peruvian Indian, a fat woman exactly like our own local women both in features and speech), (and here we began the last part of the climb, the steepest), past the field of two lanky muleteers who at some point replaced their mule with a stocky draught ox . . . My father's breast heaved not with tiredness but with insults and scoldings: we had arrived at San Giovanni, now we were on home ground.

What I ought to do now is recount every step and every gesture and every change of mood there on our land, except that everything loses its precision in my memory at this point, as if having reached the end of our climb with its rosary of images I would become wrapt in a kind of bewildered limbo, which lasted until it was time to pick up the baskets and set off down the path back home. I've already said that our daily duty consisted above all in helping father to bring back the baskets. Or rather, we were supposed to help him with everything, so as to learn how to run an estate, so as to be like him, as sons ought to be like their fathers, but soon both he and we understood that we weren't going to learn anything, and the idea of training us for the farm was tacitly dropped, or put off until we were older and wiser, as if we had been granted an extension to our childhood. Hence carrying the baskets was the only thing that was certain, the only duty accepted as undeniably necessary. The job wasn't, I should say, without its pleasure: having carefully balanced up my load, a wicker pannier on my back, a basket under one arm – with luck the other arm would be free, so the weight could be swapped about – I would set off head down, with a kind of fury, a bit like my father; and as I walked, relieved of any duty to pay attention to the world around me or to decide what to do, all my energy being employed in the effort of getting my load home and planting my feet along a path unchanging as a train track, my mind was at once protected and free to wander where it would. We plunged ourselves into this "humper's" task with exaggerated effort, myself, my brother, and my father too; since for him as for us it seemed it was no longer the

creativity of growing things, the experimenta-
tion and the risk that drew him to San Giovanni,
so much as the transportation and accumulation
of things, this antlike toiling, a question of life
or death (and in fact it almost was that now:
the interminable years of the war had begun;
amid the general penury, our family had, thanks
to the land in San Giovanni, entered a phase of
agricultural self-sufficiency, or "autarky", as
they used to say then), and if we weren't there
to help him Father would come down over-
loaded – "like a mule" was the traditional image – flaunting his burden, perhaps partly so as
to have our desertion weigh on us; but even if
one or both of his sons went with him, we would
all come down equally heavy laden, bow-legged,
mute, gazing at the ground, each absorbed in
his own thoughts, inscrutable.

Our gloom was at odds with the generous
contents of our baskets. These were concealed
(with that typical peasant diffidence towards
prying eyes) under a layer of broad vine or fig
leaves, yet with our swaying steps the loose covering would get lost along the way and the green
trunks of zucchini would emerge, the "nun's-
thigh" pears and the bunches of Saint Jeannet
grapes, the first figs, the tough down of the
chayote, the purple-green spines of the artichokes, the cobs of sweet corn to boil and

munch on, the potatoes, the tomatoes, the big bottles of milk and wine, and sometimes a spindly rabbit, already skinned, with everything being carefully arranged so that the hard things wouldn't bruise the soft and there was still enough space left for a bunch of oregano, or sweet marjoram or basil. (To my distracted eyes those baskets seemed insignificant then, as the basic materials of life always seem banal to the young, yet now that I have but a smooth sheet of white paper in their place, I struggle to fill them with name upon name, to cram them with words, and in remembering and arranging these names I spend more time than I spent gathering and arranging the things themselves, more passion . . . – no, not true: I imagined as I set out to describe the baskets that I would reach the crowning moment of my regret, and instead nothing, what came out was a cold, predictable list: and it's pointless my trying to kindle a halo of feeling behind it with these words of commentary: all remains as it was then, those baskets were already dead then and I knew it, ghosts of a concreteness that had already disappeared, and I was already what I am, a citizen of cities and of history – still without either city or history and suffering for it – a consumer – and victim – of industrial products – a candidate for consumerism, a freshly designated victim – and already the lots were cast, all the lots, our own and everybody else's, yet what was this morning fury of my childhood, the fury that still persists in these not entirely sincere pages? Could everything perhaps have been different – not very different but just enough to make the difference – if those baskets hadn't even then been so alien to me, if the rift between myself and my father hadn't been so deep? Might everything that is happening now perhaps have taken a different slant, in the world, in the history of civilization – the losses not have been so absolute, the gains so uncertain?)

The table where we laid the fruit and vegetables and filled the baskets to take back home was under the fig tree next to the old Cadorso farmhouse where the farm stewards' family lived and where the faded Masonic emblem that the old Calvinos used to put on their houses was still visible over the door. Our vineyard took up the lower part of the estate, with fruit trees planted between the rows of vines; further up were the grapefruit trees, and above them the olives. And there, in the shade of the tall, green avocado (or *aguacate*) plants, the apple of my father's eye, was the house he had built himself, the "villa" where we would live through the worst days of the war; with a model cellar and a stall for white Swiss goats on the ground floor. Our property ended at the piazza with the church of San Giovanni (where they hoisted the Cockaigne pole every twenty-fourth of June and the town band would play), then began again on the other side after a stretch of mule track, taking in a whole small valley which had a plantation of palms for funeral wreaths at the bottom, then fruit and greens further up, with a farmhouse known as Cason Bianco (where we kept sheep for a while), and a spring hidden amongst rocks green with maidenhair fern, and a limestone cavern, and a rock cave, and a fish pond, and other wonders, which were no longer wonders for me but have once again become so, now that in place of all this, stretching away in squalid and ferocious geometry, with neatly squared walls and terraces all at the same inclination, stands a carnation plantation—grey expanse of stalks in a grid of poles and wires, opaque glass of greenhouses, cylindrical cement tanks—and everything that once was is gone, everything that seemed to be there but was already only an illusion, an unaccountable stay of execution.

Since it was in the shade for part of the day, the valley of San Giovanni was at that time thought to be unsuitable for the mass cultivation of flowers and hence had preserved the traditional look of the countryside. And likewise all the farms my father walked through every morning, as if he had chosen the route on purpose to avoid the uniform, grey expanses of the carnation fields which now hemmed in the city from Poggio to Coldirodi, as if, despite working professionally in the floriculture business himself, he felt secretly remorseful about it, realized that this thing he had hoped and worked for did, yes, mean economic and technical progress for our backward agriculture, but also destruction of wholeness and harmony, loss of variety, subordination to money. And that was why he separated those hours in San Giovanni from the rest of his day, why he tried to set up a modern estate that wouldn't be hostage to a monoculture, made investments whose recovery was always uncertain, increasing the number of crops, the imported varieties, the irrigation piping, all so as to find some other way forward he could offer, one that would preserve both the spirit of the place and the drive for progress. What he wanted to achieve was a relationship with nature, one of struggle and dominion: to get his hands on nature, to change it, to mould it, while still feeling it alive and whole beneath.

And me? I imagined my mind was elsewhere. What was nature? Grass, plants, green places, animals. I lived in the midst of it and wanted to be elsewhere. When it came to nature, I was cold, reserved, sometimes hostile. I didn't realize that I too was seeking a relationship, more fortunate perhaps than my father's, a relationship that literature would give me, restoring meaning to everything, so that all at once everything would become true and tangible and possessable and perfect, everything in a world that was already lost.

Where is it my father's shouting from, telling me to bring the hose and do some watering, with everything so dry? From one strip comes the sound of old Sciaguato's fork thumping and thumping in the earth. Something is moving up in those trees: Mumina's girl has climbed up to pick a basket of cherries. I run over with the hose coiled on my shoulder, but I can't see my father amongst the rows of plants and I get the wrong strip. I have to bring the hook for pulling down the branches of the cherry tree, the sulphate dispenser, the sticky tape for grafting, but I don't know my own land, I get lost. (Now, from the vantage point of hindsight, I can see every strip, every path, now I could point out the way for myself as I run through the vines, but it's too late, everybody's gone now.)

I wish the baskets were already packed, so that we could get on home and go to the sea. The sea is over there, in a triangular cleft in the valley, V-shaped; but it's as if it were miles and miles away, the sea alien to my father and to all the people we meet on our morning walks.

Now we're walking home. I'm bowed down under my pannier. The sun is high; from the nearest paved road, on San Giacomo Hill, comes the drone of a truck; here in the valley the grey of the olives and the chuckle of the stream deaden colour and sound. On the slope opposite smoke rises from the earth: someone has lit a stubble fire. My father is talking about the way olive trees blossom. I'm not listening. I look at the sea and think I'll be down on the beach in an hour. On the beach the girls toss balls with their smooth arms, they dive into the sparkle, shout, splash, on scores of canoes and pedal-boats.

Gennaio, 1962

A CINEMA-GOER'S
AUTOBIOGRAPHY

*T*here were years when I went to the cinema almost every day and maybe even twice a day, and those were the years between '36 and the war, the years of my adolescence. It was a time when the cinema became the world for me. A different world from the one around me, but my feeling was that only what I saw on the screen possessed the properties required of a world, the fullness, the necessity, the coherence, while away from the screen were only heterogeneous elements lumped together at random, the materials of a life, mine, which seemed to me utterly formless.

The cinema as evasion, it's been said so many times, with the intention of writing the medium off – and certainly evasion was what I got out of the cinema in those years, it satisfied a need for disorientation, for the projection of my attention into a different space, a need which I believe corresponds to a primary function of our assuming our place in the world, an indispensable stage in any character formation. Of course there are other more profitable and personal ways of creating a different space for oneself: the cinema was the easiest and most readily available, and then it was also the one that instantaneously took me further away than any other. Every day, walking up and down the main street of my small town, I'd only have eyes for the cinemas, three that showed new films and changed programmes every Monday and Thursday, and a couple of fleapits with older or trashier films that changed three times a week. I would already know in advance what films were showing in all five theatres, but my eye would be looking for the posters they put up to announce the next film, because that was where the surprise was, the promise, the anticipation that would keep me excited through the days to come.

I would go to the cinema in the afternoon, slipping out of the house on the sly, or with the excuse that I was going to study with some friend or other, since during the school term my parents allowed me very little freedom. The proof of my passion was my determination to get into the theatre as soon as it opened, at two. Seeing the first showing had a number of advantages: the half-empty theatre, apparently entirely reserved for me, which meant I could lie back in the middle of the third-class seats with my legs stretched out on the back of the seat in front; the hope of getting back home without anybody realizing I'd left, so as then to get permission to go out again (and maybe even see another film); and the slight daze I would be in for the rest of the afternoon, bad for studying but good for daydreaming. Then apart from these motives, none of them things one would really want to confess to, there was a more serious one: getting into the cinema when it opened meant I was sure to enjoy the rare good fortune of seeing the film from the beginning and not from some arbitrary moment near the middle or the end as usually happened when I arrived at the cinema mid-afternoon or early evening.

Of course arriving when the film had already started was to conform with what is a barba-

rously common habit among Italian cinema-
goers, and one that still persists today. You
might say that even in those early days we Italians were looking forward to the more sophisticated narrative techniques of contemporary
cinema, breaking up the temporal thread of the
narrative and transforming it into a puzzle to
be put back together piece by piece or accepted
in the form of a fragmentary body. To console
ourselves further, I might add that watching
the beginning of the film after one had already
seen the end offered additional pleasures: that
of discovering not the resolution of the film's
mysteries and dramas, but their genesis; and
that of a confused sense of premonition vis-à-
vis the characters. Confused: in precisely the
way a clairvoyant's must be, since the reconstruction of the mangled plot was not always
easy, and would be even less so if it happened
to be a detective story, where the identification
first of the murderer and then of the crime left
an even murkier area of mystery in the middle.
What's more, there would sometimes be a bit
missing between the beginning and the end,
since suddenly looking at my watch I'd realize
I was late and that if I didn't want to incur my
parents' wrath I'd have to leave before the sequence I'd come in at reappeared on the screen.
So that many films were left with a hole in the

middle, and even today, after thirty years –
what am I saying? – almost forty, when I find
myself watching one of those old films – on tele-
vision for example – I'll recognize the moment
I walked into the cinema, the scenes I watched
without understanding, and I'll retrieve the lost
pieces and complete the puzzle as if I'd left it
unfinished only the day before.

(I'm talking about the films I saw between,
let's say, thirteen and eighteen years old, when
the cinema engrossed me to an extent far beyond
anything that came before or after; of the films
I saw in my infancy I have only confused memories, while the films one sees as an adult are
mixed up with so many other impressions and
experiences. My memories are those of one who
discovered the cinema in adolescence: I had
been kept under a tight rein as a child; for as
long as she could, my mother tried to keep me
from any dealings with the world that didn't
have a planned and obvious purpose; when I
was a small boy she rarely took me to the cinema, and then only for films that she felt were
"suitable" or "instructive". I don't have many
memories of silent films, or of the early years
of sound: a few Chaplins; a film about Noah's
ark; *Ben Hur*, with Ramon Navarro; *Dirigible*,
in which a zeppelin crashed at the Pole; the
documentary *Africa Speaks*; a futuristic film

about the year 2000; the African adventures of
Trader Horn. And if Douglas Fairbanks and
Buster Keaton hold places of honour in my
mythology it is because years later I introduced
them retrospectively into an imaginary childhood they couldn't be left out of; as a child I
knew them only from gazing at the colour posters. Generally I was kept away from films with
love stories, which in any case I couldn't understand since my unfamiliarity with film phys-
iognomy meant I was always getting the actors
mixed up, especially if they had moustaches,
and the actresses likewise, especially if they
were blondes. In the aviation films, which were
very popular when I was a child, the male characters were like so many twins, and since the
plot was always based on the jealousy between
two pilots who as far as I was concerned were
the same pilot, I would get extremely confused.
In short, my apprenticeship as a cinema-goer
was slow work and hard; which is why the passion I'm talking about exploded out of it.)

When, on the other hand, I went into the
cinema at four o'clock or five, what hit me on
coming out was the sense of time having passed,
the contrast between two different temporal dimensions, inside and outside the film. I had
gone in in broad daylight and came out to find

it dark, the lamp-lit streets prolonging the black-and-white of the screen. The darkness softened the contrast between the two worlds a little, and sharpened it a little too, because it drew attention to the passing of those two hours that I hadn't really lived, swallowed up as I was in a suspension of time, or in the duration of an imaginary life, or in a leap backwards to centuries before. Especially exciting was finding that the days had got shorter or longer: the sense of the passing seasons (always bland in the temperate clime we lived in) caught up with me as I came out of the cinema. When it rained in the film, I would listen hard to hear whether it had started raining outside too, whether I had been surprised by a downpour, having left home without an umbrella: it was the only moment when, while still immersed in that other world, I remembered the world outside; and it made me anxious. Even today, rain in films triggers the same reaction, a sense of anxiety.

If it wasn't time for dinner yet, I'd join my friends trooping up and down the pavements of the main street. I'd go back past the cinema I'd just come out of and hear lines of dialogue echoing out of the projection room onto the street, and rather than the indentification I'd felt earlier, hearing them now would instill a feeling of unreality, because by now I was firmly in the outside world, and a feeling akin to nostalgia too, as of one who turns back at a frontier.

I'm thinking of one cinema in particular, the oldest in the town and one connected with my earliest memories of the days of silent films, a cinema that had preserved from those days (and still did so right up until a few years ago) both its liberty-style street sign decorated with medals and the structure of the theatre itself, a long hall sloping downwards flanked by a corridor with columns. The projectionist's room had a small window that opened onto the main street and would blare out the absurd voices of the film, metallically distorted by the technology of the period, and all the more absurd thanks to the affectations of the Italian dubbing which bore no relation to any language ever spoken, past or future. And yet the very falseness of those voices must have possessed a communicative power all its own, like the sirens' song, and every time I passed that little window I would sense the call of that other world that was the world.

The side doors of the theatre opened onto an alleyway; in the intervals the usher with the braiding on her jacket would open the red velvet curtains so that the colour of the air outside appeared discreetly at the threshold, and the passersby and the people sitting in the cinema would look at each other a little uneasily, as though facing an intrusion equally inconvenient to both. The interval between the first and second reel in particular (another strange custom practised only in Italy and inexplicably current even today) would come as a reminder that I was still in this town, on this day at this time: and depending on how I felt, my satisfaction at knowing that in just a moment I'd be plunging back into the China Sea or the San Francisco Earthquake would grow; or alternatively I would be oppressed by this warning not to forget that I was still here, not to lose myself in far-off lands.

The interruptions in what was then the biggest cinema in the town were not so crude, since here they would change the air by opening a metallic dome at the centre of a vaulted ceiling frescoed with nymphs and centaurs. The sight of the sky in the interval would give pause for thought, with the slow passing of a cloud that might perfectly well have come from other continents, other centuries. On summer evenings the dome would stay open during the film itself; the presence of the firmament enclosed everything remote in a single universe.

During the summer holidays I could go to the cinema more freely and with less fuss. Most of my schoolfriends left our small town to go to the mountains or the country, and I would be on my own for weeks on end. Every year their departure marked the beginning of the season for hunting out old films, since the cinemas would put on things from years ago, from before the time this omnivorous craving had taken hold of me, so that in those months I could recover lost years, reconstruct a cinema-going maturity I didn't have. Films in normal commercial distribution, though: I'm not talking about anything else (exploration of the retrospective universe of the cine-club, of history consecrated and contained in the various cinematheques, would mark another phase of my life, relationships with different cities and worlds, a time when the cinema would become part of a more complex experience, of history); but in the meantime I still cherish the emotion I experienced on salvaging a Greta Garbo film that must have been three or four years old at the time but which might have been prehistoric as far as I was concerned, with a very young Clark Gable, without the moustache. *Courtesans* it was called – or was that the other? – because there were two Greta Garbo films I added to my collection in that season of revivals, though the pearl of them all was *The Blow*, with Jean Harlow.

I haven't said it yet, though I felt it would be understood, that for me the cinema meant American cinema, the Hollywood production of the time. "My" period goes pretty much from *Lives of a Bengal Lancer*, with Gary Cooper, and *Mutiny on the Bounty*, with Charles Laughton and Clark Gable, up to the death of Jean Harlow (something I went through again many years later when Marilyn Monroe died, in a decade more aware of the neurotic charge behind every symbol), with plenty of comedies in between, romantic crime movies with Myrna Loy, William Powell and Asta the dog, the musicals of Fred Astaire and Ginger Rogers, the detective stories of Chinese sleuth Charlie Chan, and Boris Karloff's horror films. I didn't remember the directors' names as well as I did the actors', but there were exceptions, like Frank Capra, Gregory La Cava and Frank Borzage, who used to feature poor people rather than millionaires, using Spencer Tracy more often than not: they were the well-meaning directors of the Roosevelt era; but that was something I discovered later; at the time, I gulped it all down without drawing many distinctions. The American cinema as it was then was composed of a gallery of actors' faces unparalleled either before or after (at least as I see it) and the plots were simple devices (amorous, character-based, generic) for bringing these faces together in ever changing combinations. Around these conventional stories there was very little flavour of a particular society or period, but that was precisely why what flavour there was struck home without my being able to define what it consisted in. It was (as I would later learn) the mystification of what lay behind that society, but it was a special mystification, unlike the Italian mystification I would be submerged in for the rest of the day. And just as a psychologist is equally interested when his patient lies as when he tells the truth, since either way he reveals something about himself, so I, as a filmgoer belonging to another system of mystifications, could learn something both from the very little truth and the great deal of mystification the products of Hollywood offered me. With the result that I bear no rancour towards that false and fabricated image of life; and although I wouldn't have been able to explain at the time, it seems to me now that I never took it as truth, but just as one of the many artificial images possible.

Of course there were some French films around too, completely different from the American productions, films that gave a greater substance to my disorientation by establishing a special link between the places I knew from experience and the places of the elsewhere (this, I would later appreciate, is what the effect known as "realism" consists in), and after seeing the Algiers Casbah in *Pépé le Moko* I would look at the streets of steps in our own old town with new eyes.

The face of Jean Gabin was made of different stuff, physiologically and psychologically, from the faces of those American actors, faces that would never look up from a table bespattered with soup and humiliation as at the beginning of *La Bandera*. (Only Wallace Beery's face in *Viva Villa* could bear comparison, and maybe Edward G. Robinson's too.) French cinema was as heavy with smells as American films were light with Palmolive, polish and antiseptic. The women had a carnal presence that established them in the film-goer's mind as at once living women and erotic fantasies (Viviane Romance is the actress I'm thinking of here), while the eroticism of the Hollywood stars was sublimated, stylized, idealized. (Even the most carnal of the American actresses of the time, the platinum-blond Jean Harlow, was made unreal by the dazzling whiteness of her skin. In black-and-white the power of the white transfigured female faces, legs, shoulders and necks, making of Marlene Dietrich not so much an immediate object of desire but desire itself, seen as some extraterrestrial essence.) I sensed that French cinema was talking about things that were more disturbing and somehow forbidden, I knew that Jean Gabin in *Quai des brumes* was not, as the Italian dubbing would have had us believe, a demobbed soldier who wanted to go and work a plantation in the colonies, but a deserter escaping from the front, something Fascist censorship would never have allowed a film to discuss.

So, I could talk for as long about the French cinema of the thirties as the American, but the discussion would digress into all kinds of other areas that have nothing to do with either the cinema or the thirties, whereas the American cinema of the thirties is entire unto itself, almost, one might say, as if it had no before and no after: certainly it has had no before or after in my life. Unlike French cinema, the American cinema of the time had nothing to do with literature: perhaps this explains why it is so separate from my experience as a whole, a profile isolated from all the rest: these cinema-going memories belong to my memories of a time before literature touched me.

What used to be called the "Hollywood firmament" formed a system entire unto itself, with its own constants and its own variables, a human typology. The actors represented models of character and behaviour; there was a hero available for every temperament; for those who aimed to tackle life through action, Clark Gable represented a sort of brutality leavened with boastful swagger, Gary Cooper was cold blood filtered through irony; for those who counted on overcoming obstacles with a mixture of humour and savoir faire, there was the aplomb of William Powell and the discretion of Franchot Tone; for the introvert who masters his shyness there was James Stewart, while Spencer Tracy was the model of the just, open-minded man who knows how to do things with his hands; and we were even given a rare example of the intellectual hero in Leslie Howard.

When it came to the actresses, the range of physiognomies and character types was more limited: the makeup, hairstyles and facial expressions tended towards a single stylization divided into the two basic categories of blondes and brunettes, and while within these two categories one might go from the spirited Carole Lombard to the practical Jean Arthur, and from the full, languid mouth of Joan Crawford to the thin, thoughtful lips of Barbara Stanwyck, what you found between those extremes was a succession of ever more indistinguishable figures, all to a certain extent interchangeable. Between the catalogue of women encountered

in American films and the catalogue of wom-
en one meets off the screen in everyday life
one could establish no connection; one might
say that where one ended the other began.
(Whereas with the women in French films the
connection was there.) From the cheeky op-
portunism of Claudette Colbert to the pungent
energy of Katharine Hepburn, the most important role model the female personalities of
American cinema offered was that of the woman
who rivals men in resolve and doggedness, spirit
and wit, this lucid self-possession in confront-
ing their male counterparts finding its most in-
telligent and ironic exponent in Myrna Loy. I
speak now with a seriousness I wouldn't at the
time have been able to ascribe to those light
little comedies; but deep down, for a society like
ours, for the Italians as they were then, especially out in the provinces, this American
woman's independence and initiative was an
instructive example, and one that to some extent got through to me. So much so that I made
Myrna Loy my prototype of the ideal feminine,
perhaps wifely, perhaps sisterly, but in any
event personifying taste and style, a prototype
that existed alongside fantasies of carnal aggression (Jean Harlow, Viviane Romance) and of
languid, extenuating passion (Greta Garbo,
Michèle Morgan), both of which kindled a de-

sire tinged with fear; or alongside that image of physical happiness and cheerful vitality that was Ginger Rogers, for whom I cherished a love star-crossed from the start, even in my daydreams, since I didn't know how to dance.

One could question whether this creation of an Olympus of women at once ideal and for the moment unattainable was a blessing or a curse for a boy. One positive aspect it did have was that it encouraged you not to settle for the little or much you actually came across, but to project your desires beyond that, into the future or the elsewhere or the arduous; the more negative aspect was that it didn't teach you to look at women with an eye eager to discover new kinds of beauty outside the established canons, or to invent new characters with what chance or quest led you to meet in your own life.

If to my mind the cinema consisted above all of actors and actresses, one should nevertheless remember that for me, as for all Italian moviegoers, only half of each actor and actress was truly present, in the sense that we got only their bodies and not their voices, which were substituted by the abstraction of the dubbing, by a conventional, alien, insipid diction, no less anonymous than the printed subtitles which in other countries (or at least in those where filmgoers are thought to be more mentally agile) tell you what the mouths nevertheless continue to communicate with all the considerable charge of individual pronunciation, of a phonetic signature made up of lips, teeth, saliva, made up above all of the varying, geographically conditioned accents of the American melting pot, in a language that for those who understand it offers nuances of expression and for those who don't brings with it an extra musical potency (such as one hears today in Japanese and Swedish films). The conventionality of American cinema was thus "dubbled" (you will excuse the almost pun) by the conventionality of the dubbing, which to our ears, however, became part and parcel of the film's enchantment, something inseparable from the images, a sign that the power of the cinema was born silent, and that sound – at least for Italian cinema-goers – has always been felt as an appendage, a caption in block capitals. (The Italian films of the time, for that matter, although not dubbed, might just as well have been. And if I don't mention them here, despite having seen and still remembering almost all there were, it's because, for better or worse, they made so little impression, and hence there is simply no place for them in an essay presenting the cinema as another dimension of the world.)

In my determination to see as many American films as I could, there was more than a little of the collector's doggedness, so that every role played by an actor or actress was like a postage stamp in some series I was gradually sticking down in the album of my memory, painstakingly filling in the gaps. So far I have mentioned only the famous stars, male and female, but my collector's enthusiasm went beyond them to the scores of supporting actors who were a necessary ingredient of any film at that time, particularly for the comic parts (Everett Horton and Frank Morgan), or the "baddies" (John Carradine and Joseph Calleia). It was a bit like in the pantomime, where all the roles are predictable, so that reading the cast list I would already know that Billie Burke must be the somewhat dotty lady, Aubrey Smith the crusty colonel, Mischa Auer the penniless scrounge, Eugene Pallette the millionaire; but I would also look forward to the little surprise, of recognizing a well-known face in an unexpected role, wearing different makeup perhaps. I knew almost all their names, right down to the actor who always played the touchy hotel porter (Hugh Pagborne), and the one who was always the barman with the cold (Armetta); and where I've forgotten names, or never managed to find them out, I still remember the faces; of the various butlers, for example, who formed a category all their own in the cinema of the time, and a very important one too, perhaps because people had already begun to realize that the age of the butler was over.

But my erudition you must remember is the erudition of the simple film-goer, not the expert. I would never be able to compete with the erudite professionals in the field (nor even appear on quiz shows) because I have never been tempted to fill out my memories by consulting handbooks, film catalogues and specialized encyclopedias. These memories form part of a mental storehouse where what matters is not written documents but the casual deposition of images across days and years, a storehouse of private sensations I have never wanted to mix up with the storehouses of the collective memory. (Of the critics of the time I used to read Filippo Sacchi in the *Corriere*, very smart and alert to my favourite actors, and, later, "Volpone" in *Bertoldo*, who turned out to be Pietro Bianchi and was the first to establish a bridge between cinema and literature.)

I ought to say that this whole business lasted only a few years: my enthusiasm barely had time to reach self-awareness and escape from parental repression before it was suddenly suffocated by the repression of the state. All at once (1938, I think), in order to extend its self-sufficiency to the film industry, Italy introduced an embargo on American films. It was not, properly speaking, a question of censorship: as in the past, the censor continued to give or not give his approval to this or that individual film, and those that didn't get it were never seen and that was the end of the matter. No, despite the clumsy anti-Hollywood campaign launched at the same time as the embargo (this was precisely the moment when the regime's propaganda machine was falling into line with Nazi racism), the real reason for the measure was one of commercial protectionism, of creating space on the market for Italian (and German) productions. As a result, the four big American producers and distributors Metro, Fox, Paramount and Warner (as I said, I'm writing from memory, trusting in the exactness with which my mind recorded the trauma) were kept out, while films made by other American producers, such as RKO, Columbia, Universal and United Artists (which even before the embargo had been handled by Italian distributors) were still shown right up to the end of 1941, right up to the moment, that is, when Italy found itself at war with the USA. So I was still granted the occasional isolated treat (indeed, one of the biggest: *Stagecoach*), but my collector's voracity had been mortally wounded.

Of course, when compared with all the other prohibitions and obligations that fascism had imposed, and the even tougher ones it was now imposing in those prewar years and would later impose during the war, the banning of American films was a minor, even minimal deprivation, and I was not so foolish as not to appreciate this: but it was the first to strike directly at me, who knew no other regime than fascism, nor had felt any needs other than those that the world I lived in had been able to prompt and satisfy. It was the first time that a right I enjoyed had been taken away from me: more than a right, a dimension, a world, a mental space; and I experienced this loss as a cruel oppression, one which contained within it all the forms of oppression that I knew about only from hearsay or from having seen others suffer. And if I can still speak of it today as of a blessing lost, it is because something went out of my life then never to return. By the time the war was over, so much had changed: I had changed, and the cinema had changed, changed in itself and changed in relation to me. My cinema-going biography resumes but it is that of a different cinema-goer, who is no longer just a cinema-goer.

With so many new ideas going through my head, whenever I thought back to the Holly-

wood cinema of my adolescence, it would seem
a rather poverty-stricken affair: it hadn't been
one of those heroic eras of the silent cinema,
or the introduction of sound, for which my first
explorations of film history were now whetting
my appetite. My memories of life during those
years had changed too, and so many things that
I had thought of as routine and insignificant
were now dense with meaning, tension, premonition. In short, thinking back over my past,
the world of the screen appeared much paler,
more predictable, less exciting than the world
outside it. Of course, I might always say that
it was the dullness and banality of provincial
life that pushed me toward those celluloid
dreams, but that would be to resort to a cliché
that oversimplifies the complexity of the experience. There is no point in my explaining here
how and why the provincial life going on about
me in my childhood and adolescence was in fact
made up entirely of exceptions to the norm, how
the sadness and listlessness, if such they were,
lay inside me and not in the outward appearance
of things. Even fascism, in a small place where
one never grasped the mass dimension of phe-
nomena, was a collection of separate faces, of
individual attitudes, hence not a uniform man-
tle like a layer of tar but rather (I speak of the
disenchanted viewpoint of a boy looking half

from without and half from within) another
contrasting element, a piece of the puzzle which
because of its unusual shape was more difficult to fit in with the other pieces, a film
whose beginning I had missed and whose end
I couldn't imagine. So what had the cinema
meant to me in this context? I suppose: distance. It satisfied a need for distance, for an
expansion of the boundaries of the real, for
seeing immeasurable dimensions open up all
around me, abstract as geometric entities, yet
concrete too, crammed full of faces and situations and settings, which established an (abstract) network of relationships with the world
of direct experience.

Since the war, cinema has been seen, dis-
cussed, made, in a completely different way. I
don't know to what extent postwar Italian cinema has changed our way of seeing the world,
but it has certainly changed our way of seeing
the cinema (any cinema, even American cinema). We no longer have one world within the
brightly lit screen in the darkened theatre, and
another heterogeneous world outside, the two
being divided by a clean break, an ocean or
abyss. The darkened theatre disappears, the
screen becomes a magnifying glass placed on
the routine world outside, forcing us to focus
our attention on what the naked eye tends to

skim over without settling on. This function has – can have – its usefulness, marginal, more substantial or occasionally very considerable. But it does not satisfy that anthropological and social need for distance.

At this point (to pick up the thread of individual biography) I quickly got involved in the world of the printed page, which along one margin or another borders on the world of celluloid. Immediately, I had the vague impression that, for the sake of my old love of the cinema, I must preserve my condition of spectator pure and simple, that I would lose the privileges that came with that condition if I were to join those who made the films: and anyway I was never tempted to try. But since Italian society is fairly restricted, one ends up sitting next to film directors in the trattoria, everybody knows everybody, and this takes away a great deal of the fascination of being a cinema-goer (and a reader). Add to that the fact that Rome for a while became an international Hollywood, and that the barriers between the film worlds of the various producing countries soon came down, and it's obvious that every aspect of the old sense of distance was lost.

But I still keep going to the cinema. The exceptional encounter between spectator and filmed vision is always a possibility, whether thanks to art or to chance. In the Italian cinema one can expect a great deal from the personal genius of the directors, but very little from chance. This must be one of the reasons why I have sometimes admired and frequently appreciated Italian cinema, but never loved it. I feel it has taken more from my pleasure of going to the cinema than it has given. For such pleasure has to be assessed not just in terms of the "art films" with which one establishes a critical relationship of the "literary" variety, but also with regard to whatever may or may not be coming out of the middle- and low-brow productions, with which one tries to re-establish the relationship of someone who goes to the cinema purely to watch.

Thus I ought to talk about the satirical comedy of manners which dominated middle-brow Italian cinema throughout the sixties. But in most instances I find it detestable, since the more ruthless its caricature of our social behaviour pretends to be, the more self-satisfied and indulgent it actually becomes; occasionally I do find it genial and lighthearted, informed by an optimism that has remained miraculously genuine, but then I don't feel it helps us to make any progress toward self-knowledge. The fact is, looking ourselves in the eyes is no easy matter. Italian vitality quite rightly enchants foreigners, and equally rightly leaves me cold.

It is scarcely a coincidence that Italian cinema developed a homegrown product of consistent quality and originality of style only when it turned to the western, that is, when it rejected the dimension on which Italian cinema had founded its reputation and become bogged down, when it constructed an abstract space, a parodic distortion of a purely cinematographic convention. (But in this way it also says something about us, our mass psychology: about what the western means to us, about how we integrate and adjust the myth so as to invest our hopes and fears in it.)

In the same way, I too have to leave the Italian context if I am to rediscover the pleasure of the cinema, have to become once again a pure spectator. In the tiny, smelly studios of the Latin Quarter I can dig out the films of the twenties or thirties, films I thought I had lost forever, submit myself to the onslaught of the most recent productions from Brasil maybe, or Poland, films from worlds I know nothing about. That is, either I go looking for old films that tell me about my own prehistory, or those that are so new as perhaps to suggest what the world will be like after me. And again, it is always the American film – I'm talking about the most recent ones – that have something absolutely novel to tell us: and as always that novelty has to do with the highways, the drugstores, young faces or old, the way one moves through spaces, the way one passes one's life.

But it isn't distance that the cinema gives us now: it is the irreversible impression that everything is nearby, is hemming us in, is on top of us. And this close-up observation can be of an exploratory-documentary kind or an introspective kind, these being the two directions in which the cognitive function of today's cinema can be described as operating. One gives us a strong image of a world outside ourselves that for some objective or subjective reason we are not able to perceive directly; the other forces us to see ourselves and our daily existence in a way that changes something in our relationship with ourselves. For example, Federico Fellini's work very closely approximates my own cinema-goer's biography, which Fellini himself recently convinced me to write; except that for him biography has become cinema, it is the outside world that invades the screen, the dark of the theatre turned inside out in the cone of light.

The autobiography Fellini has been developing without a break from *I Vitelloni* on is special to me not just because he and I are almost the same age, and not just because we both come from seaside towns, his on the Adriatic, mine in Liguria, where the lives of idle young boys were pretty similar (although in many ways my San Remo, being a border town with a casino, was different from his Rimini, and for us the contrast between the summers and the "dead season" of winter was perhaps only really felt during the war years), but because behind all the wretchedness of the days in the café, the walks to the pier, the friend who dresses in woman's clothes and then gets drunk and weeps, I recognize the unsatisfied youth of the cinema-goer, of a provincial world that judges itself in relation to the cinema, in a constant comparison between itself and that other world that is the cinema.

In this sense, the biography of the Fellini-esque hero – which the director starts over again every time – is more exemplary than my own in that his young man leaves the provinces, goes to Rome and crosses over to the other side of the screen, making films, becoming himself the cinema. A Fellini film is cinema turned inside out, the projector that swallows up the public and the camera that turns its back to the set, but the two poles are still interdependent, the provinces acquire meaning by being remembered in Rome, Rome acquires meaning in having arrived from the provinces, and between the human monstrosities of the one and the other, a common mythology is established, a mythology that revolves around gigantic female deities like the Anita Ekberg of *La Dolce Vita*. What Fellini's work strives to do is bring this feverish mythology to light and classify it. And at the heart of that work, like a spiral crammed with archetypes, stands the self-analysis of 8½.

To get a more exact picture of what happened, one must bear in mind that the role reversal from cinema spectator to cinema director was preceded in Fellini's life by that of the reader of humorous weeklies turned illustrator and contributor to the same. The continuity between Fellini the illustrator-satirist and Fellini the director is evident in the character of Giulietta Masina and in all that special "Masina area" of his work, that is, in a rarefied lyricism that assimilates the figurative schematization of the humorous cartoons, and reaches out – through the small-town piazzas of *La Strada* – to the world of the circus and the melancholy of the clown, one of the most insistent motifs in the Fellini repertoire and one of those closely tied to a stylistic taste which was already given, I mean which corresponds to a childish, disembodied, pre-cinematographic way of visualizing a world that is "other". (That "other" world on which the cinema confers an illusion of embodiment, thus confounding its phantoms with the attractive-repulsive carnality of life.)

It is no accident that the film which analyses the world of Masina, *Giulietta degli spiriti*, has its declared figurative and chromatic point of reference in the colour cartoons of *Corriere dei Piccoli*: it is the graphic world of the mass-market printed page which here reasserts both its special visual authority and the close relationship it has had with the cinema right from the start.

Within this world of graphics, the humorous weekly, which I suspect is still virgin territory to sociologists (far as it is from the beaten tracks of Frankfurt and New York), really ought to be studied, since it is almost as indispensable a departure point as the cinema for understanding the popular culture of provincial Italy between the wars. Also to be studied (if it hasn't already been) is the link between the humorous weeklies and the Italian cinema, if for no other reason than for the role it has in the biography of another and older of the founding fathers of our cinema: Zavattini. It is the contribution of the humorous weeklies (perhaps more than those of literature, figurative art, sophisticated photography and Longanese-style journalism) which provides the Italian cinema with a tried and tested form of mass communication functioning through figurative and narrative stylization.

But as film director, Fellini's relationship with the comic weeklies is not just with the "poetic", "crepuscular" and "angelic" side of their humour, to which his cartoons and early articles subscribed, but also with the more plebeian and Roman slant typical of other cartoonists at the *Marc'Aurelio* – Attalo, for example, who represented the society of the time with such nastiness and determined vulgarity, such a coarse and impudent deftness of line, as to exclude every illusion of consolation. The power of the image in Fellini's films, which is so difficult to define because it cannot be placed within the codes of any figurative art, has its roots in the extravagant and discordant aggression of these journalistic cartoons. It's the same aggression that lies behind the triumph of a certain kind of cartoon and comic strip worldwide, in the sense that the more individual these cartoons are in terms of style, the more capable they become of communicating to a wider public.

This underlying capacity to communicate with the public is something Fellini has never lost, even after the language of his films becomes more sophisticated. Likewise the determined anti-intellectualism of his work has never let up: as Fellini sees it, the intellectual is always a hopeless case who may at best hang himself, as in 8½, and who when he loses control, as in *La Dolce Vita*, shoots himself after having first killed his children. (The same choice in *Roma* is taken in the time of classical stoicism.) Fellini has stated that his intention is to contrast the intellectual's arid, reasoning lucidity with a magical, spiritual knowledge springing from religious participation in the mystery of the universe: but on looking at the results, my own impression is that neither of the two comes over with sufficient emphasis in the cinema. What we do have, on the other hand, as a constant defence against intellectualism, is the sanguine nature of Fellini's instinct for spectacle, the elemental, carnival, end-of-the-world truculence that both his modern and ancient Romes never fail to evoke.

What has so often been defined as Fellini's baroque style consists in his constantly forcing the photographic image along the road that leads from the caricatural to the visionary, while always keeping in mind the departure point of a well-defined subject of representation which must seek out its most communicative and expressive form. For those of us who are his contemporaries, this is particularly evident in his images of fascism, which, however grotesque the caricature, always have the flavour of truth. Over two decades fascism generated as many different psychological climates as, with every new year, it did uniforms: and Fellini always gets the right uniforms and the right psychological climate for the years he is representing.

Faithfulness to the truth ought not to be a criterion of aesthetic judgement, and yet on looking at films by the new generation of directors who like to reconstruct the Fascist period indirectly, as a historical-symbolic scenario, I can hardly help but cringe. Particularly in the work of the most prestigious of our young film-makers, everything that has to do with fascism is always wide of the mark, justifiable conceptually perhaps, but false at the level of the image, as if the man never managed to hit a bull's-eye even by accident. Does this mean that the experience of a historical period cannot be transmitted, that a fine fabric of perceptions is inevitably lost? Or does it mean that since the images the young use to conjure up Fascist Italy are mostly drawn from writers (from ourselves) and are fragmentary in nature, presupposing an experience that was once common property, they are unable to evoke the historical density of the period now that this shared reference has been lost? In Fellini, by contrast, we need only see the boys in the train blowing raspberries at the ridiculous stationmaster of *The Clowns* and him calling over a black-moustached railway militiaman and the boys' arms coming up out of the ghostly train in a silent Roman salute, and the atmosphere of the period is completely and unmistakably restored to us. Or we need only hear the lugubrious sound of the air-raid siren wailing across the little variety theatre of *Roma*, and the effect is the same.

Probably the same result of precise evocation through extremes of caricature can likewise be found in the images of a religious education which appears to have constituted a fundamental trauma in Fellini's life, considering how frequently he presents us with terrifying priests of a positively physiological horror. (But I am not in a position to judge authenticity here: the only repression I was subjected to was secular, more internalized and less easily shaken off.) As a counterbalance to the image of a repressive church-as-school, Fellini offers us the vaguer image of church-as-mediator in the mysteries of nature and man, a church without distinct features, like the dwarf nun who calms the madman on the tree in *Amarcord*, a church which offers no answers to man's tortured questions, like the ancient monsignor who speaks about the birds in 8½, certainly the most intriguing and unforgettable image of Fellini's religious side.

Thus Fellini can go far indeed along the road of visual repugnance, but along that of moral repugnance he stops short, he recuperates the monstrous into the human, into the indulgent complicity of the flesh. Both the well-fed province and the movie-making world of Rome are circles of hell, but at the same time enjoyable lands of Cockaigne as well. That is why Fellini manages to disturb us to the core: because he forces us to admit that what we would most like to distance ourselves from is what is intrinsically close to us.

As in the analysis of neurosis, past and present perspectives become confused; as in the outbreak of an attack of hysteria, they are exteriorized in spectacle. Fellini turns the cinema into a symptomatology of Italian hysteria, that special family hysteria which prior to Fellini was represented as a mainly southern Italian phenomenon and which he, from the geographical middle ground of his Romagna, redefines in *Amarcord* as the one true unifying element of Italian behaviour. The cinema of distance which nourished our youth is turned forever on its head in the cinema of absolute proximity. For the brief span of our lifetimes, everything remains there on the screen, distressingly present; first images of eros and premonitions of death catch up with us in every dream; the end of the world began with us and shows no signs of ending; the film we thought we were merely watching is the story of our lives.

MEMORIES OF
A BATTLE

*I*t's not true that I've forgotten everything, the memories are still there, hidden in the grey tangle of the brain, in the damp bed of sand deposited on the bottom of the stream of thought: assuming it's true, that is, that every grain of this mental sand preserves a moment of our lives fixed in such a way that it can never be erased yet buried under billions and billions of other grains. I am trying to bring a day, a morning, back to the surface, moments between dark and light at the dawning of that day. It's years since I stirred up these memories, lurking like eels in the pools of the mind. I was sure that whenever I wanted I had only to poke about in the shallows to see them rise to the surface with a flick of their tails. At most I would have to lift one or two of the big stones that form a barrier between present and past to uncover the little caves behind the forehead where things forgotten lie low. But why that morning? Why not another? Here and there bumps protrude from the sandy bottom, suggesting that a sort of vortex used to whirl around them, and when memories awake after a long sleep it is from the centre of one of those vortices that time's spiral unravels.

Yet almost thirty years later, now that I've finally decided to haul in memory's nets and see what's inside, I find myself groping in the dark, as if that morning didn't want to begin again, as if I were unable to unglue the sleep from my eyes, and perhaps it is precisely this imprecision that guarantees that the memory is precise, what now seems half erased was so then too, that morning they woke us at four, and immediately the Olmo detachment was on the march down through the woods in the dark, almost running through shortcuts where you can't see where you're putting your feet, not paths at all perhaps, just steep gorges, beds of dry streams overrun by brambles and ferns, smooth pebbles your hobnail shoes slither on, and we're still at the beginning of the approach march, just as it's an approach march I'm trying to make now on the trail of memories that crumble under pressure, not visual memories because it was a moonless starless night, memories of my body slithering in the dark, with half a plate of chestnuts in my stomach that haven't warmed me up and are just weighing me down like an acid handful of gravel that squeezes and jolts, with the weight of the machine-gun ammunition box banging on my back and every time my foot slips there's the danger the thing will topple me facedown on the ground or pull me over backwards my back against the stones. Maybe all that's left in my memory of the whole descent are these falls, which could equally be those of some other night or dawn. Morning marches before action are all the same, I'm one of the group carrying ammunition for my squad, always humping that hard square box with the straps that dig into my shoulders, but in this memory my curses and those of the men behind me are kept down to a crackle of whispers, as if our moving in silence were the key factor this time even more so than other times, because at the same moment on the same night lines of armed men like our own are coming down along all the ridges in the wood, all the detachments of the Figaro battalion billeted in hidden farm-houses have set out on time, all the battalions of Gino's brigade are pouring down from the valleys, and along the mule tracks they run into other lines on the march since the evening be-fore from mountains far away, since the mo-ment they got that order from Vittò, who's commanding the division: all partisans of the area to gather at dawn around Baiardo.

The air is slow to brighten. Yet it should be March by now, spring should be beginning, the last (can it be true?) of the war or the last (for how many more of us?) of our lives. The un-certainty of the memory is surely the uncer-tainty of the light and the season and what was to follow. The important thing is that this de-scent into an uncertain memory swarming with shadows should lead me to set foot on something solid, as when I felt the crushed stones beneath my feet, and recognized that stretch of the big road to Baiardo that goes past the bottom of the cemetery, and at the turn, even though I can't see it, I know that opposite us is the village rising to a point at the top of the hill. Now that I have wrenched a specific place from the shad-ows of my forgetfulness, a place I've known since childhood, immediately the darkness be-gins to grow transparent letting shapes and colours filter through: all of a sudden we're not alone any more, our column is marching alongside another column stopped along the road, or rather we're walking between two lines like our own shuffling their feet, their rifles propped on the ground. "Who are you with?" someone asks us. "With Figaro. And you?" "With Pelletta." "We're with Gori," names of commanders with bases in other valleys, other mountains.

And passing by we watch each other, because it's always strange when one unit meets another, when you see how many different things we are all wearing, clothes of every colour, odd bits of uniforms, but how recognizable and alike we are too, the same tears where our clothes tend to come apart (where the rifle strap rests on the shoulder, where the brass magazines wear out the pockets, where branches and bushes have torn our trousers to shreds), alike and unlike in the weapons we have, a sad collection of battered old "ninety-ones" and German hand grenades with their wooden handles tucked in our belts, in the midst of which the eye settles on examples of light, faster, more modern weapons that the war has scattered across the fields of Europe and that every battle redistributes on one side and the other. Some of us are bearded, some callow, long-haired or shorn, with the spots you get from eating nothing but chestnuts and potatoes for months on end. We size each other up coming out of the dark as though surprised to find that so many of us have survived the terrible winter, to see so many of us together as happens only on days of great victory or great defeat. And unanswered in our eyes as we look at each other are our questions about the day that is dawning, a day being planned in a back-and-forth of commanders with binoculars round their necks hurriedly sorting out the squads along the dusty road, deciding positions and assignments for the attack on Baiardo.

Here I should open a parenthesis to tell you that this village of the Maritime Pre-Alps, clinging to the rocks like an old castle, was held at the time by the Republican *bersaglieri*, students for the most part, a well-armed, well-equipped, well-trained body of men controlling the whole olive-green valley right down as far as Ceriana, and that for months a ferocious unrelenting war had been going on between us partisans of the "Garibaldi" brigades and these *bersaglieri* of Graziani's army. I would have to add all kinds of other things to explain what the war was like there in those months, but rather than awakening memories this would bury them again under the sedimentary crust of hindsight, the

without pincers. I even remember the battle plan, how it was supposed to unfold in various phases, and how it didn't unfold. But to follow the thread of my story I'll have to remember it all through my ears: the special silence of a country morning full of men moving in silence, rumblings, shots filling the sky. A silence that was expected but that lasted longer than expected. Then shots, every kind of explosion and machine-gun fire, a muddle of sound we can't make sense of because it doesn't take shape in space but only in time, a time of waiting for us stationed at the valley bottom where we can't see a damn thing.

I continue to gaze into the valley bottom of the memory. And my fear now is that as soon as a memory forms it immediately takes on the wrong light, mannered, sentimental as war and youth always are, becomes a piece of narrative written in the style of the time, which can't tell us how things really were but only how we thought we saw them, thought we said them. I don't know if I am destroying the past or saving it, the past hidden in that besieged village.

The village is up there, near and unapproachable, a village where there wasn't very much worth capturing in the end, but which for us nomads out in the woods for months had become the focus of notions of home, streets,

people. A girl evacuee who the previous August
(when we held Baiardo) had looked at me in
amazement on recognizing me among the partisans. You see, memories of war and youth
couldn't help but include at least one woman's
glance, in the middle of the village besieged in
its circle of death. Now the circle is just isolated
shots. An occasional burst of fire still. Silence.
We are on the alert, ready to cut off some lost
enemy. But nobody comes. We wait. However
things have gone, surely now one of our people
will come to get us. We've been here a long
time on our own, cut off from everything.

Again it's sound, not sight, that holds the
reins of this memory: from the village comes a
din of voices, singing now. Our boys celebrating
victory! We head towards the village, almost at
a run. We're right by the first houses already.
What are they singing? It's not "*Fischia il vento
. . .*" We stop. It's "*Giovinezza*" they're singing!
The Fascists have won. Immediately we leap
down through the olive terraces, trying to put
as much distance as we can between us and the
village. Heaven knows how long our lot have
been retreating already. Heaven knows how we
are going to catch up with them. We've been
left stranded in enemy territory.

My memories of the battle end here. Now
all I can do is cast about for my memories of

the flight over a carpet of hazelnuts along the dry streambed we try to climb up to avoid the roads, go back and make my way once again through the night and the woods (a human shadow ran across our path, seized by panic it seemed, we never found out who), sift through the cold ashes of the deserted camp trying to find traces of the Olmo squad.

Or I could bring into focus everything I later found out about the battle: how our men ran into the village shooting and were pushed back leaving three dead. And immediately I try to describe the battle in a way I didn't see it, the memories that have so far lingered behind vague shadows suddenly pick up speed and direction: I see the column opening up the way to the piazza while the others who went around the village are climbing the steps of the narrow streets. I could give them all their names, their places their gestures. Memories of what I didn't see in the battle take on a more precise order and sense than what I really experienced, because free from the confused sensations that clutter my memory of the whole. Of course even here there are blanks I can't fill. I concentrate on the faces I know best: Gino is in the piazza: a thickset boy commanding our brigade, he looks into the square and crouches shooting from a balustrade, black tufts of beard round his tense jaw, small eyes shining under the peak of his Mexican hat. I know that Gino had taken to wearing a different hat at the time but I can't remember now if it was a bearskin or a wool cap, or a mountain cap.

I keep seeing him with that big straw hat that belongs to a memory of the previous summer.

But there's no time left for imagining details because the boys have to get out fast if they're not to be trapped inside the village. Tritolo jumps forward from a low wall and throws a grenade as if he were playing a joke. Cardù is near him covering the others as they retreat, waving to them to say the way is clear now. Some of the *bersaglieri* have already recognized the Milan squad, ex-comrades of theirs who came over to us a year ago. And here I'm getting close to the point that's been on my mind right from the beginning, the moment when Cardù dies.

This imagined memory is actually a real memory from that time because I am recovering things I first imagined back then. It wasn't the moment of Cardù's death I saw, but afterwards, when our men had already left the village and one of the *bersaglieri* turns over a body on the ground and sees the reddish-brown moustache and the big chest torn open and says, "Hey, look who's dead," and then everybody gathers round this dead man who instead of being the best of theirs had become the best of ours, Cardù who ever since he had left them had been in their thoughts, their conversation, their fears, their myths, Cardù who many of them would have liked to emulate if only they'd had the courage, Cardù who carried the secret of his strength in that calm bold smile.

Everything I've written so far serves to show me that I remember almost nothing of that morning now, and there would be other pages to write to tell of the evening, the night. The night of the dead man in the enemy village watched over by the living who no longer know who is living and who is dead. My own night as I search for my comrades in the mountains to have them tell me if I have won or if I have lost. The distance that separates that night then from this night I'm writing in now. The sense of everything appearing and disappearing.

LA POUBELLE
AGRÉÉE

When it comes to housework, the only task I can perform with a certain amount of competence and satisfaction is that of taking out the rubbish. The operation involves a number of stages: removal of the kitchen bin and emptying of the same into the larger bin in the garage, then transportation of the said larger bin to the pavement outside the front door, where it will be picked up by the dustbin men and itself emptied into their truck.

The kitchen bin is a cylindrical bucket made

of a plastic material which is pea-green in colour. Before taking it out one has to wait for the right moment, when it can be assumed that everything there was to throw away has been thrown away, that is when, having cleared the table, the last bone or peel or crust has slipped down off the smooth surface of the plates, and the same rapid gesture of expert hands has arranged those plates, after a first quick rinse under the tap, in neat columns in the racks in the dishwasher.

Kitchen life is based on a musical rhythm, on a concatenation of movements, like dance steps, and when I speak of rapid gestures, it's a female hand I think of, not my own clumsy sluggish movements, that's for sure, always getting in the way of everybody else's work. (At least that's what I've been told my life long by parents, friends – male and female – superiors, underlings and even my daughter these days. They've been conspiring together to demoralize me, I know; they think that if they go on telling me I'm hopeless they'll convince me there's an element of truth to the story. But I hang back on the sidelines, waiting for an opportunity to make myself useful, to redeem myself.)

Now the plates are all caged up in their little carriage, round faces astonished to find themselves standing upright, curved backs waiting for the storm about to break over them down there at the bottom of the tunnel where they will be sent off in exile until the cycle of cloud-bursts, waterspouts and steam jets is over. This is the moment for me to go into action.

Here I am, then, on my way downstairs already, holding the bucket by its semicircular handle, taking care that it doesn't swing too much and spill its contents. The lid I usually leave behind in the kitchen: it's an irksome accessory, that lid, it never quite manages to combine its two tasks of concealing the rubbish and of getting out of the way when you have some more to chuck in. The compromise one settles for involves keeping it at an angle, a bit like a mouth opening, trapping it between the bucket and the wall in precarious equilibrium, so that it winds up on the floor, with a dull bang, not unpleasant to the ear, like a vibration that's been restrained, since plastic doesn't vibrate.

I ought to say that here in Paris we're living in a one-family home (to use a less than attractive but understandable contemporary locution), or a *pavillon* (to put it in a French at once timeless and still rich with suggestive connotation). This so as to explain the different sense of my ritual gestures with respect to those performed by the condominium owner or tenant in a big block of flats who gets rid of his daily rubbish by emptying it from the family *poubelle* into the communal *poubelle*, which is usually located in the courtyard of the building and which at the appropriate time the porter's wife will put out on the street thence to be entrusted to the care of the council refuse collection service. That transfer from one container to another, which for most inhabitants of the metropolis takes on the significance of a passage from private to public, for me in our house, in the garage where we keep the big *poubelle* during the day, is only the last gesture of the ceremonial upon which the private is founded – and as such is accomplished by myself as paterfamilias – my taking leave of the leftovers of things confirming their complete and irreversible appropriation.

It must be said, however, that the big *poubelle*, despite being undeniably our own private property, having been purchased in regular fashion on the open market, already looks, in terms of its shape and colour (a dark green, military-uniform grey), like a piece of official city equipment, and proclaims the role that the public sphere, civic duty and the constitution of the polis play in all our lives. Our choosing it was not in fact the result of the arbitrariness of aesthetic taste, or of our experience in its practical use, as happens with other household objects, but was dictated by respect for the city's bylaws. Wisely, these laws prescribe the features and dimensions such *poubelles* must have in order that their daily deployment along the city streets not be offensive to the eye (uniformity tends to pass unobserved), or to the sense of smell (the lid, as long as the rubbish is not overflowing, ought to close around the top of the drum with its profiled edge, in such a way that neither the wild leap of the cat in heat nor the methodic sniffing of the dog can knock it off), or to the ear (replacing the old metal version, the soft plastic muffles any clashing sounds, thus protecting the townsfolk's sleep when in the uncertain light of dawn the dustbin men get down to the business of pulling off the lids and dragging away the bins to tip them up into their ghostly trucks).

It's no accident that the exact name of this kind of container, the name used by the customer who wishes to buy it in a general store and by the shopkeeper who sells it to him, is the *poubelle agréée*, which is to say a pleasing dustbin, something approved and acceptable (with the implication: approved by prefectorial regulations and by the authority that is made outwardly manifest in them and that is inwardly present in the individual consciences of the citizens, thus founding the basis of our social contract and of the expediencies of good living). One should remember at this point that in the expression *poubelle agréée* it is not just the adjective that bears the seal of paternal metropolitan bureaucracy, but the substantive that comes before it. *Poubelle*, a common noun describing an object, recalls the proper name of a person: it was a Monsieur Poubelle, Prefect of the Seine, who first ordered (in 1884) the use of these containers in the hitherto polluted streets of Paris.

With the result that when I empty the small bin into the big one and lift it up by its two handles to carry it out of our front door, though still functioning as a humble cog in the domestic machine, I am nevertheless already taking on a social role; offering myself as the first link in a chain of operations crucial for collective cohabitation, I am confirming my dependence on the institutions without which I would die buried under my own rubbish in the snail shell of my individual existence, at once introverted and (in more than one sense) autistic. Such is the departure point for proper clarification of the reasons that make my *poubelle* truly *agréée*: acceptable in the first place to me, even if not pleasant, as one has to accept the unpleasant without which none of what pleases us would have any sense.

I do recall other ways of getting rid of rubbish: having lived in big apartment blocks, I know the dull sound the contents of a bin make when they rush through the vertical disposal ducts, plummeting down and down to the dark vaults at courtyard level: a procedure that combines an agile exploitation of gravity – the first beneficiaries of which were doubtless the prehistoric lake dwellers – with the system, adopted even earlier by the cavemen, of heaping things up in remote ravines, and one that brings with it the well-known drawbacks of evil-smelling accumulations whenever the shaft gets blocked.

Going further back in time, the San Remo of my childhood springs to mind, and I see the dustbin man with his sack on his back walking up the hairpins of the drive as far as the villa to collect the rubbish from the zinc bin: our genteel lifestyle seemed guaranteed for all eternity by the availability of cheap labour.

Meanwhile, in the endless residential suburbs of individualistic, prosperous, democratic, industrial civilization, thousands of identical little people came out of identical little houses, each complete with little garden and garage, to place thousands of identical bins in line on the pavements: an Anglo-Saxon image that goes back to the dawn of the society of the masses, but which in my memory is associated with my first trip to America, when I was still living in a fluid, floating bachelor anarchy in which household duties were certainly the last thing on my mind, and it was Barolini who spoke to me then of the rule of taking out the "garbage can" every day as being one of the key elements underpinning domestic life in Croton-on-Hudson. (The father of an exemplary American family – the family was American, not him – he had immersed himself in his role late in life and tended to observe himself from outside as he acted his part.)

"The *garbagio*," he would say in his Anglo-Veneto, as if to impress his chore firmly in his mind, "I mustn't forget to take out the *garbagio*." The voice of my dead friend has been coming back to me ever since I became a father myself, and likewise of a foreign family, not in a green suburb of New York but in a densely populated suburb at the gates of Paris (but can it really be Paris? I look out from a little house more Londonish than Parisian onto a secluded court-yard that people call the *Square*, more maybe because of the vague sense of disorientation it inspires than because of the green you see condensed in stunted lilacs along the walls) ever since I too started putting out the "garbage can", or *poubelle agréée*, in front of the gate.

It was no doubt his obedience to Christian precepts which brought my friend to accept this rule quite happily. And me? I would like to be able to say, with Nietzsche, "I love my destiny," but I can't do that until I have explained for myself the reasons that lead me to love it. Carrying out the *poubelle agréée* is not something I do without thinking, but something that needs to be thought about and that awakens the special satisfaction I get from thinking.

Every word we think oscillates in a mental field where different languages intrude. Shoving aside the French, the English verb *to agree* invades the field: it is in order to respect an *agreement*, a pact settled by the mutual consent of the parties involved, that I am placing this object out on this pavement, with all that the international use of the English word implies.

An *agreement* with whom? With the city, of course, to which I pay my annual *taxe d'enlèvement des ordures ménagères* and which undertakes to relieve me of this burden every day of the year – including Sundays and excluding only a few high holidays – just so long as I make the first move, namely, carry my regulation bin to this threshold at the regulation time. And in this respect I have already committed a first breach of contract, in that it is forbidden to leave rubbish out in the street during the night if it is not to be picked up before the morning: but an article of law so inhuman as to oblige me to wake before first light I feel justified in interpreting with a certain latitude, as though in a tacit *agreement* (there we are), especially since I live in a place where hardly anyone goes by, where a nocturnal encumbrance on the pavement does not impede the public passage. And then partly because the stronger unwritten law to which the ritual of our daily habits bows dictates that expulsion of the day's rubbish coincide with the winding up of the same day, and that one go to sleep after having removed from the house any possible sources of unpleasant smells (as soon as the evening's visitors are gone, quick, open the windows, rinse the glasses, empty the ashtrays; in the *poubelle* the layer of ash and stubs puts its seal on the accumulation of the day's detritus the way in geological sections glacial deposits separate one era from another) not just out of a natural concern for hygiene but so that on waking up the following morning one may begin the new day without having to touch what the evening before we cast off from ourselves forever.

Taking out the *poubelle* should thus be interpreted simultaneously (since this is how I experience it) as a contract and as a rite (two notions that can be brought into even closer unity in so far as every rite is a contract, but for the moment I don't want to press ahead – contract with whom? – quite that far), a rite of purification, the abandoning of the detritus of myself, and it doesn't matter whether we're talking about the very detritus contained in the *poubelle* or whether that detritus refers us back to every other possible detritus of mine; what matters is that through this daily gesture I confirm the need to separate myself from a part of what was once mine, the slough or chrysalis or squeezed lemon of living, so that its substance might remain, so that tomorrow I can identify completely (without residues) with what I am and have. Only by throwing something away can I be sure that something of myself has not yet been thrown away and perhaps need not be thrown away now or in the future.

The satisfaction I get out of this, then, is analogous to that of defecation, of feeling one's guts unburdening themselves, the sensation at least for a moment that my body contains nothing but myself, and that there is no possible confusion between what I am and what is unalterably alien. Alas the unhappy retentive (or the miser) who, fearing to lose something of his own, is unable to separate himself from anything, hoards his faeces and ends up identifying with his own detritus and losing himself in it.

If this is true, if the gesture of throwing away is the first and indispensable condition of being, since one is what one does not throw away, then the most important physiological and mental gesture is that of separating the part of me that remains from the part I must jettison to sink away into a beyond from which there is no return.

It is thus that the purificatory rite of *enlèvement des ordures ménagères* can also be seen as an offering made to the underworld, to the gods of death and loss, the fulfillment of a vow (which brings us back to our contract). The content of the *poubelle* represents the part of our being and having which must daily sink away into darkness so that another part of our being and having may remain behind to enjoy the light of day, may truly be and truly have. Until the day when the last support of our being and having, our physical body, itself becomes dead detritus to be laid on the cart that leads to the incinerator.

Thus this daily representation of descent below ground, this domestic and municipal rubbish funeral, is meant first and foremost to put off my own personal funeral, to postpone it if only for a little while, to confirm that for one more day I have been a producer of detritus and not detritus myself.

Hence that state of mind at once gloomy and euphoric which one associates with carrying out the rubbish; and the way we see the men who go by emptying the bins into their pulping truck not just as emissaries of the chthonic world, gravediggers of the inanimate, Charons of a beyond of greasy paper and rusty tin, but as angels too, as indispensable mediators between ourselves and the heaven of ideas in which we undeservedly soar (or imagine we soar) and which can exist only in so far as we are not overwhelmed by the waste which every act of living incessantly produces (even the act of thinking: these thoughts of mine that you are reading being all that has been salvaged from the scores of sheets of paper now crumpled up in the bin), heralds of a possible salvation beyond the destruction inherent in all production and consumption, liberators from the weight of time's detritus, ponderous dark angels of lightness and clarity.

All it takes is for the dustbin men to go on strike for a few days leaving the rubbish to pile up at our doorways, and the city is transformed into a corrupted dunghill; far more quickly than anyone could have predicted we are being suffocated by our incessant production of refuse, the technological armour of our civilization turns out to be a fragile shell; medieval visions of decadence and pestilence open up once more before us.

This is particularly true of Italy, and emblematic of a history that has been one long crisis. Bad government spreads outward through our town councils along a hundred paths both evident and obscure but it is always in the innermost recesses of the Refuse Disposal Department that scandal explodes uncontrollably. It's as if something basically wrong were revealing itself in our relationship with our rubbish, some profound defect in the Italian mind, or rather the Catholic-Italian mind, given that shipwrecks in these particular waters are a feature of Christian Democrat administrations, perhaps due to a religious error, of moral theology and of faith too, a misguided sense of how much should be left to Providence and how much is the responsibility of man, an underestimation of the sacred nature of the operations involved in refuse removal (as in every other civic service), their considering material necessity not as an area for choice and trial but as a burden which ever since the Fall we have been able to do naught else but bear and in relation to which every shortcoming is but a venial sin to be passed over with indulgence since we will in any event be cleansed of it at the last without any justification being required beyond a gesture of formal piety (or at the civic level a vote for the right party, or faction within the party). As a result of which the ranks of our "Municipal Sanitation Staff" (a bureaucratic neologism which immediately jettisons the notion of practical service in favour of the limbo of belonging to some unspecified clerical administration) can swell beyond all limit and without regard to the council budget in order to guarantee wage packets to a plethora of hangers-on who will never be initiated into the infernal and angelic trials of the mission with which nominally they have been invested. While that great purifying instrument, the essential guts of the city, the incinerator, is profanely seen as just another opportunity for the customary kickbacks taken from council contracts and suppliers, without our being awed by its symbolic importance, without seeing ourselves judged by the looming machine, without enquiring how much of ourselves we fear or hope may be reduced to ashes.

One has to say, however, that in Paris strikes by the *éboueurs* are no less frequent (*éboueurs* is the official name, which is to say, mud removers, this in memory of an unimaginable Paris of muddy streets rutted by carriage wheels and fouled with trodden horsedung), a result of the perpetual discontent of a recently immigrated work force obliged to accept the lowliest and heaviest of jobs without proper contracts. Drawing a comparison with Italy, one could say that the reasons are the opposite but the results are the same: in the precarious Italian economy, the position of dustbin man is defended as a stable occupation, a job for life; in the solid French economy, refuse collection is a precarious occupation, performed by those who have not yet managed to put down roots in the city and susceptible to regulation only through the reciprocal threats of unemployment and strike.

It is a characteristic of demons and angels that they should present themselves as strangers, visitors from another world. Thus the *éboueurs* materialize in the morning mists, lineaments refusing to detach themselves from the indistinct: earthy complexions – the North Africans – a sprinkling of whiskers, cap on head; or – those from black Africa – just the whites of their eyes lighting up faces lost in the dark; voices that superimpose sounds inarticulate to our ears over the muffled roar of the truck, sounds that bring relief when they filter into your morning slumber reassuring you that you can go on sleeping a little while longer because others are out there working for you. The social pyramid goes on shuffling its ethnic strata: the Italian labourer in Paris is driving his own truck now, the Spaniard has become a skilled worker, the Yugoslav a bricklayer, the lowliest labourer is Portuguese, and when you get to the man shovelling earth or sweeping the streets it is always a clumsily decolonized Africa that raises its sad eyes from the city pavement, but without catching your own, as if an insuperable distance still separated us. And in your sleep you sense that the dustcart isn't just grinding refuse, but human lives too and social roles and privileges and it won't stop until it has done the whole round.

You only have any direct contact with the dustbin men just before Christmas when they come to bring you their cardboard calendar which says, *Messieurs les Eboueurs du 14ème Vous Souhaitent une Bonne et Heureuse Année*, and to pick up their tip. For the rest of the year the communication between us and them lies in the contents of the *poubelle*, a rich source of information indeed if anyone chose to consider them day by day: the empty bottles after party evenings, the wrapping paper from the shops where we've bought things, the pages full of crossings-out where a writer has racked his brains over his essay on *poubelles*. Loading the dustcart, the immigrant in his first job discovers the city as one might look at the wrong side of a carpet: he judges the wealth or the poverty of the different areas from the quality of their refuse, which then stimulates his dreams of the consumer's destiny that awaits him.

Here we arrive at the economic crux of what I have hitherto chosen to refer to juridically as a contract and symbolically as a rite: my relationship with the *poubelle* is that of the man for whom throwing something away completes or confirms its appropriation, my contemplation of the heap of peels, shells, packaging and plastic containers brings with it the satisfaction of having consumed their contents, while for the man who unloads the *poubelle* into the rotating crater of the dustcart it offers only an idea of the amount of goods which are denied to him, which reach him only as useless detritus.

But perhaps (and here my essay glimpses an optimistic conclusion and immediately succumbs to the temptation), perhaps this denial is only temporary: his having been taken on as a dustbin man is the first step up a social ladder that will eventually make today's pariah another member of the consumer society and like everybody else a producer of refuse, while others escaping from the deserts of the "developing countries" will take his place loading and unloading the bins. Thus the *poubelle* will be *agréée* for him too, for the North African or the Negro who lifts it to the mouth of the evil-smelling grinder in the morning fog, thus the grinder itself will prove not just the final destination of the industrial process of production and destruction but also the point from which one starts again from scratch, the entry point into a system that swallows up men and remakes them in its own likeness and image.

From here our argument can follow one of two diverging paths: a history of the pariah's satisfied integration as he moves towards the conquest of Paris from the furthest frontier of the refuse dumps; or a history of revolution and the overturning of that mechanism, at least in the mind, a spreading outward of the vibrations of the truck stopped beneath my windows so far as to tremble the settled foundations of centuries of Western civilization. But both visions (both illusions) are reunited in this *poubelle*, agreeable to all of us but even more so to the anonymous economic process that multiplies new products fresh out of the factory and likewise their wornout remains to be thrown away, leaving us, the dustbin man and I, with the sole task of lifting up this container to fill and to empty. In the rite of throwing away, we would like, the dustbin man and I, to rediscover the promise of that cyclical completion peculiar to the agricultural process, in which – so they say – nothing was lost: what was buried in the earth sprouted up again. (There – once an essay sets off on an evocation of the archaic, who will ever be able to stop it?) Everything happened in the simplest and most regular of fashions: after their subterranean sojourn, seed, manure and sacrificial blood returned to the light with the new harvest. Of course industry multiplies its goods more than agriculture but it does so through profits and investments: the plutonian realm that has to be crossed in order for the metamorphosis to take place is the cave of money, capital, the City of Dite, inaccessible to myself and the dustbin man (privatized or state-employed though he may or shall be: by now we know that the distinction has little importance), presided over by a Supreme Board of Directors who are no longer plutonian but hyperuranium, and who deal in the abstraction of numbers whose values are enormously remote from the sticky and fermenting terrestrial melting pot to which the dustbin man and I entrust our sacrificial offerings of empty jars, our seedings of wastepaper, our participation in the arduous breakdown of synthetic materials. In vain do we pour out, the dustbin man and I, our dark cornucopia, the recycling of the leftovers can be no more than a practical accessory that does not modify the substance of the process. The pleasure of having perishable things (consumer goods) sprout again remains a privilege

of the god Capital who turns the soul of those
things to money and in the most favourable of
circumstances leaves us their mortal remains
for our use and consumption.

But how can I infer what the man from Africa thinks and sees on emptying my *poubelle*?
It's myself I'm talking about, only and always
myself, it's my own mental categories I'm ap-
plying as I seek to understand the mechanism
of which I am (of which we are) a part, even
though we do have a common point of departure:
our escape from and rejection of a primitive
agricultural system now in a state of crisis.
When once abundant harvests fail and famine
starves the fields, the farming man – say eth-
nologists – is overcome by distress and remorse
and looks for a way to expiate his guilt. I don't
know if this is true for the *éboueur* (perhaps the
fellah has no memory of a time without famine;
perhaps the disciple of Islam is immune to guilt
complexes); but it is certainly true in my case:
the remorse I carry around with me since childhood is still that of the landholder's son who in
disobedience to his father's wishes has left the
estate in alien hands, rejecting the luxuriant
mythology and severe moral code in which he
was educated, the abundance and variety of
fruits that only the proprietor-farmer's assidu-
ous presence in the fields together with a single-

minded stubbornness, and then efficiency and initiative in trying out new crops and techniques, can wring from the earth.

And in this kitchen in the heart of the metropolis where my long flight has brought me, my old drama is still acting itself out. Every family is business, or rather *hacienda*, place of activity, place of physical and cultural survival through a system of shared labour, place where a cycle, albeit limited, of food production and consumption is enacted. And it is the rules governing my behaviour in this elementary *hacienda* that I am seeking to establish now, to set out in a contract or "agreement", it is in order that I may be privately *agréée* that I am manoeuvring a *poubelle* that is publicly *agréée*, myself *agréée* in the domestic context, in the tacit distribution of household tasks, in the orchestration of the daily suite that is family existence.

Here I am, then – hang on a moment – going down to empty the *poubelle*. The *poubelle* is the instrument that serves to bring me into a harmony, to get me in tune with the world and the world in tune with me. (So the contract concerns no one but myself, it is a mutual agreement between me and myself, me and my interior law, or Kantian imperative, or superego.) But this harmony is impossible. Having taken its slow course for half a century or more, the long Crisis of the Bourgeois Family is now precipitating into its convulsive phase with the Disappearance of the Last Housemaids, ultimate prop of the institution. The division of labour between equals (as between the bear hunter and his wife the bear cooker in the primordial cave) seems to be inextricably (since the beginning of time perhaps) connected to the division of labour between unequals (masters and servants): so much so that with the latter now a matter of controversy, the former likewise turns out to be impracticable. The message, whether explicit or tacit, that the Chorus of Western Women addresses to the Chorus of Men, in this twilight of our millennium, goes like this: "I can cook once for a party, once to express myself, once to pass on a tradition, once out of necessity, and once for love, but I will not cook three hundred and sixty-five days a year just because it has been decided that my role is that of cooking and yours that of sitting down to eat." Something fundamental has changed in the collective consciousness, but since almost nothing has changed when it comes to our actual habits, the result is a constant cloud of discontent. The man, however big a contribution he may make to the family budget, is seen as a parasite if he fails to contribute to the housework. Perhaps we will arrive at a new

modus vivendi, a redistribution of roles; or perhaps no system of compensation is possible now,
either inside or outside the family. Perhaps in
the future not even a restaurant will let you get
away with merely paying your bill; you'll have
to help peel the potatoes first and wash the
dishes afterwards.

The kitchen, which should be the happiest
place in the house (NB: when I copy out this
page, I mustn't forget to put in an attractive
description here: the sparkling wall units, the
hum of electrical appliances, the lemony smell
of the detergent for the cutlery), is now seen
by women as a place of oppression and by men
as a place of remorse. The simplest solution
would be the interchangeability of roles: hus-
band and wife cook together, or take turns, or
one partner cooks while the other does the
cleaning, or vice versa. But the fact is that this
solution is hampered by prejudice (and here I
leave our universal discussion to return to the
presentation of the individual case of my own
daily experience) in the sense that the others
consider me so incapable of handling oven and
burners that no sooner do I stand there ready
to do something than everybody else moves away
telling me that what I'm doing is wrong or
clumsy or pointless or even dangerous. Like all
prejudices, this one is easy to pass on: my

daughter is still a little girl, but if we're alone together in the kitchen she is already finding reasons for criticizing everything I do and saying she prefers to do it all herself (after which she will give a detailed account of my shortcomings to her mother). And just as such a lack of faith in my capacities has always discouraged me from learning, so it discredits me as a possible teacher: thus does the knowledge accumulated over generations approach me only to pass me by and exclude me.

None of the above would matter if I didn't feel that this deficiency of mine were considered a crime, and related to other things I do that are likewise criminal. If I can't cook it's because I'm not worthy to cook (this is the burden of the argument against me and it weighs heavily), as the unworthy alchemist can never obtain gold nor the unworthy knight win the joust. Even my attempts to pitch in are frowned upon, seen not as a demonstration of goodwill but as hypocrisy, a smokescreen, a histrionic exhibition. I cannot save myself by Works, but only by the Grace which has not and will not be conceded. If I manage to make an omelette, it is not the first step towards progress and interior growth: no, because there's no way that's a Real Omelette, it's a forger's hoax, a charlatan's trick. Cooking is God's trial, something I have failed once and for all, undeserving of initiation. All I can do is seek out other ways to justify my presence on this earth.

Without false modesty, I think I can say that the field of action that best suits my talents is that of transportation. Going from one place to another, transporting an object, be it heavy or light, for distances either long or short: whenever I find myself in this situation I feel at peace with myself, as one who is able to attribute usefulness, or at least a goal, to his actions, and for as long as the journey lasts I experience a rare sensation of inner freedom, my mind wanders far and wide, my thoughts soar upward. I am happy, for example, to "run errands", to go and buy bread, butter, greens, the paper, stamps. I say "run errands" so as to establish a continuity between these duties I now have as head of the household and those that used to be entrusted to me when I was a boy: I could say "do the shopping", but this would imply initiative, choice, risks: assessing and comparing ever higher prices, discussing cuts of meat with the butcher, picking up ideas from the products on display, the greens, the early fruit from abroad, the cheeses. Of course "doing the shopping" is what I would most enjoy, at least in theory; in practise I can't hope to compete with those who move about the shops much more naturally than I do, with such sharpness of eye, such experience and imagination, such practical sense and personal flair. Hence it's wiser for me to limit my relationship with the marketplace to emergency stopgap expeditions: carrying a piece of paper with a list of the things I have to ask for (*"un grand pot de crème fraîche"*) and their weight (*"une livre de tomates"*), and sometimes even the price, just as when they sent me "to run errands" as a boy.

In Paris the shopping basket hangs mainly from male hands, or at least that's how it looks to an Italian used to seeing the shops in his own country mostly frequented by women, and here one gets back to appreciating how carrying food is the primary duty in home management. So that my agricultural past resurfaces now in a metropolitan context, and I recall the image of my father laden with baskets, proud to be carrying the produce of his land back home with his own hands, as a sign of his feeling that he was "master", first and foremost in the sense of "master of himself", of his self-sufficient, Robinson Crusoe independence, an independence even in respect to those paid hands whom he would resort to only for what he couldn't do with his own or with those of his ever reluctant sons.

Is it, then, the mule track of the rejected

farmer's vocation that I retrace in my memory as I walk along this street in the Fourteenth Arrondissement, between the grocer's and the baker's and the greengrocer's? No, it's another road, which I used to walk as an adolescent: the one that took me from our villa to the town, when being sent to "run errands" was a pretext for getting out of the house, and sometimes I would pretend I had forgotten something so as to be able to go out again. But more often than not I didn't even need to pretend, I was so scatterbrained and so uninterested in the real purpose of my trip, and they would have to repeat what I was supposed to buy and its weight and price over and over to get it into my head, and count out the exact money for me.

It was a short-range Mercury who guided my steps and who still guides them today, partial reflection of the god who mediates and connects the profusion of the world, and who, unfortunately, only rarely rewards my devotion by illuminating me with his full silvery light. Or, when I am going down towards the gods of the underworld, towards the murky recesses where life's leftovers are tossed away, it's the psychopomp Mercury who walks before me, guiding my burden of dead weights down to the banks of the municipal Acheron.

I come back to the kitchen with the small
bin empty and replace the sheet of newspaper
still lining it with a fresh sheet of newspaper.
I particularly enjoy this little job because I am
happy to find a further use for the newspapers,
to allow them an extra lease on life beyond their
instant obsolescence. Object of an unsatisfied
love, or just a neurotic obsession, the newspaper
is something I always buy, leaf through quickly
and then put away, but it upsets me to throw
it out right away, I am always hoping that it
may prove useful later on, may still have something to tell me. The moment of resurrection
comes, of course, when I pull out a sheet from
the heap of old newspapers to line the *poubelle*
and headlines appear all creased up in the concave perspective of the bucket demanding an
immediate second reading as I arrange the rec-
tangular surface of the paper to cover the inside
of the cyclinder as best it can, tucking in the
flaps around the rim. The *Le Monde* format is
ideal for the little bin, while the larger Italian
dailies usually end up lining the big *poubelle*. If
carefully applied, the newspaper lining will still
be sticking to the container after it has been
emptied by the *éboueurs*, and tomorrow, when
I go to recover my empty *poubelle*, this large
pavis of writing in the language of Dante will

enable me to distinguish my bin from its other sister *poubelles* abandoned on the same pavement.

I've been writing this piece on and off for three or four years now, and since I started there have been all sorts of changes in, amongst other things, the way *poubelles* are managed. The newspaper lining is already a thing of the past: like everybody else, I'm now using those plastic bags that have transformed the image of urban rubbish, hiding it away in smooth shiny wrappings, a step forward that I hope no one, no matter how nostalgic for the past or hostile to plastic, will want to criticize, even if the rubbish does continue to be recognizable as such despite its packaging and the heaps on the pavements in the days when we have a *grève des éboueurs* are no less putrid. (On the contrary, I would say that whatever it really contains, even the brighest plastic bag makes us think of rubbish these days, since it is always the stronger image that asserts itself over the more anodyne.)

Another fundamental reform: the kitchen sink drain has been fitted with a *broyeur*, or waste disposal unit, which can chop up a considerable amount of food leftovers (excluding, curiously, artichoke leaves, whose fibres get stuck in the unit's teeth and clog it up), so that our rubbish has changed too, in the sense that it contains less organic waste.

And then, we have replaced the kitchen bin too, the green one, with a new one made of white plastic which has a lid you raise and lower with a pedal and contains a bucket you can lift out. So that now it's only the bucket I carry down and empty in the big bin, or rather, not even the bucket, but the bag – again plastic – that I pull out of the bucket, replacing it with a new one. (There's an art to getting the bag to stick to the rim of the bucket, holding it so that it grips all round and won't slip down, but then you have to get out the air left underneath which lifts the bottom, blowing it out like a sail.)

The full bag, on the other hand, I tie up with the tape provided on the bottom of the bag: a clever idea, this tape, and, like every small invention that simplifies life's difficulties, welcome. (There's an art to tying an overfull bag while simultaneously holding it up in the air, this because you have to pull it out of the bin to pull off the tape, and once it is out you don't know where to put it down or how to prevent the rubbish from spilling out onto the floor.) So now I carry off this bag tied with a bow like a

Christmas present and drop it into the big *poubelle*, which, once again, is lined with a big grey plastic bag.

Of course these won't be the last developments in the long series of transformations our habits have undergone and will undergo as we adapt to the times, always assuming that our times themselves don't end. The reform that seems to be most pressing and important will be that of separating the rubbish according to its qualities and different destinies, incineration or recycling, so that at least part of what we have wrung from the treasures of the world may not be lost forever but discover the path of regeneration and re-use, the eternal return of the ephemeral.

One of the materials that could run out and whose salvaging is of particular concern to me, is paper, fond daughter of the forest, living space of the writing and reading man. I realize now that I should have begun this piece by distinguishing and comparing two types of domestic rubbish, cooking leftovers and writing leftovers, the rubbish bin and the wastepaper basket. And distinguishing and comparing the different destinies of what cooking and writing do not throw away, the products themselves, in one case something eaten, assimilated in our bodies, in the other something that, once finished, is no longer a part of me and of which it is impossible to say whether it will become food for another's reading, for a mental metabolism, or what transformations it will undergo in passing through other minds, how many of its calories it will transmit and whether it will set them in circulation again, and how. Writing, no less than throwing things away, involves dispossession, involves pushing away from myself a heap of crumpled-up paper and a pile of paper written all over, neither of the two being any longer mine, but deposited, expelled.

All that's left to me and belongs to me is a sheet of paper dotted with a few sparse notes, on which over the last few years under the title *La Poubelle Agréée* I have been jotting down the ideas that cropped up in my mind and that I planned to develop at length in writing, *theme of purification of dross   throwing away is complementary to appropriating   the hell of a world where nothing is thrown away   one is what one does not throw away   identification of oneself   rubbish as autobiography   satisfaction of consumption   defecation   theme of materiality, of starting again, agricultural world   cooking and writing   autobiography as refuse   transmission for preservation* and still other notes whose thread and connective reasoning I can no longer make out, *theme of memory   expulsion of memory   lost memory*

*preserving and losing what is lost   what one hasn't
had   what one had too late   what we carry around
from the past   what does not belong to us   living
without carrying around anything from the past (animal): perhaps one carries around more   living for
the work one produces; one loses oneself: there is
the work that doesn't work, I am no longer there.*

[*Paris, 1974–76*]

FROM THE OPAQUE

*I*f they had asked me then what shape the world is, I would have said it is a slope, with irregular shifts in height, with protrusions and hollows, so that somehow it's as if I were always on a balcony, looking out over a balustrade, whence I see the contents of the world ranged to the right and to the left at various distances, on other balconies or theatre boxes above or below, a theatre whose stage opens on the void, on the high strip of sea against the sky crossed by winds and clouds

———

and likewise if they ask me now what shape
the world is, if they ask that self that dwells
within me and preserves the first impression of
things, I shall have to answer that the world is
arranged on so many balconies irregularly de-
ployed so as to look out over one great balcony
that opens on the void of the air, on the win-
dowsill that is the short strip of sea against the
vast sky, and the real self within me is still
looking out from that parapet, the real self
within the presumed inhabitant of worldly
shapes more complex or more simple but all
derived from this shape, shapes far more complex and at the same time far more simple since
all are contained or can be deduced from those
first sudden drops and slopes, from that world
of lines oblique and broken amongst which the
horizon is the only continuous straight line.

So I shall begin by saying that the world is
made up of broken and oblique lines, with seg-
ments that tend to protrude from the corners
of each level, like the agave plants that often
grow along the brink, and with vertical ascending lines like the palm trees that shade

gardens and terraces above those where they are rooted,

and I refer here to the palms of the past when palms would usually be high and houses low, the houses likewise cutting vertically across the line of the shifts of height, standing half on the level below and half on the level above, with two ground floors one below and one above, and likewise even now that houses are usually higher than any palm tree, and trace longer vertical ascending lines amid the oblique and broken lines of the ground levels, it is still true that they have two or more ground floors and that however high they may rise there is always a ground level higher than their roofs,

with the result that in the shape of the world I am now describing the houses appear as if one were looking down on their roofs from above, the city is a tortoise down there at the bottom, its chequered shell in relief, and this not because I am not accustomed to seeing houses from below, on the contrary I can always close my eyes and sense the houses behind me tall and oblique without depth almost, but in that case it takes only a single house to conceal the other possible houses, I can't see the city higher up and I don't know if it is still there, every house above me is a vertical board painted pink and resting on the slope, all the depth flattened in one direction but without expanding in the other, the properties of space vary according to the direction I am looking in with relation to my particular orientation

Obviously to describe the shape of the world the first thing to do is to establish my position, I don't mean my location but my orientation, because the world I am talking about differs from other possible worlds in this sense: that whatever the time of day or night one always knows where east and west are, and thus I shall begin by saying that I am looking southwards, which is the same as saying that I have my face towards the sea, which is the same as saying that I have my back to the mountain, because this is the position in which I usually surprise that self that dwells within myself, even when my external self is orientated in a completely different fashion or not orientated at all as is often the case, since for me every orientation starts from that initial orientation, which implies my always having the east to my left and the west to my right, and only by setting out from there can I locate myself in relation to space, and verify the properties of space and its dimensions

So if they had asked me how many dimensions space has, if they asked that self which still does not know the things one learns so as to have a code of conventions in common with others, and first among these the convention according to which each of us stands at the meeting point of three infinite dimensions, skewered by one dimension that goes in through the chest and out from the back, by another that runs through us from shoulder to shoulder, and by a third that pierces the skull to come out from the feet, an idea one accepts only after considerable resistance and frequent rejections, but then pretends to have always known because everybody else is pretending to have always known it, if I were to answer on the basis of what I had really learnt by looking around me, about the three dimensions which with standing in the middle of them turn out to be six dimensions, in front behind above below right left, by observing them as I was saying with my face to the sea and my back to the mountain,

the first thing to say is that the in-front-of-me dimension does not exist as such, since immediately below me there opens the void, which then becomes the sea which then becomes the horizon which then becomes the sky, so that one might even say that the in-front-of-me dimension corresponds to the above-me dimension, to the dimension which comes out from the centre of all our skulls when we're standing upright and which is immediately lost in the empty zenith,

then I would pass on to the behind-me dimension which never goes far behind because it encounters a wall a cliff a rugged or bushy slope, since I always have my back towards the mountain which is to the north, hence I might say that even this dimension doesn't exist as such or gets confused with the subterranean dimension of the below, with the line that supposedly comes out from under your feet and which of course doesn't come out at all since between the soles of your shoes and the floor-

boards below there simply isn't the space for it
to come out,

and then there is the dimension that extends
to the left and the right and which for me corresponds more or less to the east and the west,
and this dimension may indeed proceed on both
sides as the world proceeds with its jagged out-
line in such a way that at every level one can
trace an imaginary horizontal line that cuts the
oblique inclination of the world, a line like those
that are traced on altimetric maps and that go
by the splendid name of isoheight

or like the water sluices that direct the
meagre flow of the streams into horizontal
ditches to irrigate the strips of arable land on
slopes to either side of the hill, strips won from
the land by supporting the terrain with stone
walls

but even in this dimension one can't really
go very far because sooner or later whether it
be to the east or the west one reaches the watershed of a headland at which either one can

think of the line as losing itself in the air of the sky thus blending in with the first dimension we spoke of,

or one can have it continue on the far side like a good isoheight following the series of inlets and bays and the hollows within these inlets and bays, until it encounters promontories that advance further into the sea than other promontories, defining larger bays which enclose the inner bays, and so on and on until we have established that this pattern of inner bays and other bays, golden in the morning and blue in the evening to the west, greenish in the morning and grey in the evening to the east, goes on like this for the entire length of the seas and the continents, stretching out to enclose the whole sea in a single bay,

so that one may as well take the shape of the world to be that of the bay I have before my eyes, defined by the headland to the east of me and the headland to the west of me, and if not by a headland then by whatever it is that limits my vision to one side and the other, ridge of a hill, trunk of an olive tree, cylindrical surface of a cement tank, juniper hedge, araucaria, sunshade, or whatever happens to form the two curtains that define the stage upon which I find myself, a tall backdrop behind me, the footlights of a bright horizon in front

I've gone back to using metaphors that have to do with the theatre, although in my thoughts of that time I couldn't have associated the theatre and its velvets with that world of grasses and winds, and although even now the image that the theatre tends to bring to mind, that is of an interior that claims to contain within itself the exterior world, the piazza the fête the garden the wood the pier the war, is the exact opposite of what I am describing, that is an exterior that excludes every kind of interior

a world all outside which gives us the impression of being closed inside while being outside, since one person's piece of ground looks out over another person's piece of ground, these being divided not by boundary walls but by support walls, and each of us in his own piece but looking at the others each in their own, and no one ever leaving his own yet always under the gaze of the others, a space which is exterior even when it is within an interior, hen coops rabbit hutches appearing behind metal fences, booths pergolas shelters gazebos, each pool reflecting what is above the pool, outside stairways connecting roof terraces where basil grows on windowsills in pots full of earth, a village is a pinecone all arches and windows, the window frames the dresser across whose mirror a cloud passes

One would also have to say so as to dispel every equivocation the word theatre might give rise to, that the theatre is made in such a way that the maximum number of eyes can enjoy the maximum freedom of vision, in such a way that is that all possible vision is contained and directed as though within a single eye looking at itself, seeing itself mirrored in the iris of its own pupil,

while I speak of a world where everything can be seen and can't be seen at the same time, in so far as everything sprouts and hides and protrudes and screens, the palms open and close like a fan on the masts of the fishing boats, the jet of a hose shoots up and waters a field of invisible anemones, half a bus turns in the half-bend of the drive and disappears amongst the spikes of the agave plant,

   my gaze is shattered amongst different planes and distances, runs along an oblique strip of matting and greenhouse glass, touches a field all bristling with strings and sticks on the slope opposite, returns shortening to the close-up of a leaf hanging from the branch of a medlar tree in the middle here, moves from the cloud of a grey olive tree to a white cloud sailing in the sky, then right under my eyes enormous and green with sulphur is a tomato plant in a scaffolding of canes, then a small pantiled roof the other side of the stream where a line of persimmon trees begin, with yellowish red fruit on the branches which I can count even at this distance

   and equally one would have to define what a theatre is in terms of sounds, a place of maximum audibility, a great ear that holds all vibrations and notes within itself, an ear listening to itself, at once ear and shell held to ear, while I on the other hand am speaking of a world where sounds break up as they ascend and descend the convolutions of the terrain and skirt around sharp corners and obstacles, soften and spread of their own accord from the distance, the conversation between two women meeting in the middle of a street of steps is lost no sooner than it rises above the baskets they carry on their heads, but the oohs, the aahs, the dear me's are audible on the hillside opposite coming through the air like beads running down the thread of a necklace, space is formed of visible points and sound points constantly mixing together and never quite managing to coincide,

and it's only at night that the sounds find their place in the dark, measure out their distances, the silence that they carry around them describes the space, the blackboard of the dark is dotted and sketched with sound, the speckling of a barking dog, the softly shaded collapse of an old palm frond, the dotted line of the train erased a little then emphasized a little as it enters and leaves the tunnels, and no sooner has the sound of the train gone than there's the sea coming out like a white shadow at the point where the train disappeared, you hear it for half a minute and then no more,

and already the far and nearby cocks are hurrying to trace out the horizon that frames all the sounds drawn in the dark, before the sponge of the dawn smudges the blackboard from one corner to the other, and in the daylight you can't tell where any of the sounds are coming from any more, the squeak of the sulphur sprayer gets tangled up with the roar of the motorbike, the drone of the electric sawmill hems in the tinkle of the merry-go-round, to the person watching from a stationary position the world flakes away fitfully before eye and ear in the landslide of space and time.

To the person watching from a stationary position the only constant element is the curve the sun describes as it rises and sets from left to right, and even where there is no sunshine we always know where the sun is, and of every thing whose distance and shape we cannot determine we can always know how the shadow at its feet moves shrinks stretches, of every colour whose colour we can't define we can always

predict how its colour will change according to
the angle of the sun's rays,

in the end the sun is no more than the relationship the world has with the sun, which
does not change if one considers the concave
curve the sun describes as a convex curve, it is
the relationship between a source of light rays
no matter whether mobile or fixed with a body
or amalgam of bodies no matter whether fixed
or mobile which receives those rays, that is the
sun consists of the properties of the rays the
world receives from it, rays that supposedly
originate from a source known as the sun which
blinds you if you stare at it, and which needs
only a tatter of cloud to hide away behind, only
a few intervening layers of denser atmosphere
or water vapour to grow paler and fog over to
the point that it disappears, or even just a little
mist rising from the sea, so that in any case it
is not the hypothetical existence of this source
that matters but the manner in which its rays
fall on the surfaces of the world, either directly
varying in intensity inclination frequency, or
indirectly along variable angles of reflection,
and depending on whether they are reflected by
the dazzling mirror of the sea or by the ash-
grey earth and stones of the coast, as when in

a bay the western shore is deserted by a sun that has already set but receives the reverberation of a still sunlit east

or instead of considering the source of the rays or the rays themselves or the surfaces that receive them, one might consider the dapple of shadows the places that is that the rays do not reach, how the shadow sharpens in proportion to the strength of the sun, how the morning shadow of a fig tree from being tenuous and uncertain becomes as the sun climbs a black drawing of the green tree leaf by leaf expanding at the plant's foot, that concentration of the black to signify the polished green the fig tree encloses leaf by leaf on the side turned towards the sun, and the more the drawing on the ground concentrates its blackness the more it shrinks and shortens as if sucked in by the roots, swallowed up by the foot of the trunk and returned to the leaves, transformed into white sap in their veining and stalks, until at the moment when the sun is at its highest the shadow of the vertical trunk disappears and the shadow of the umbrella of leaves curls up beneath, on the fermented squashiness of the ripe figs that have fallen to the ground, waiting for the shadow of the trunk to sprout out again and push it towards the other side lengthening out there as if the gift of growth, which the fig tree as fruit-bearing plant has renounced, passed to this ghost plant stretched out on the ground, until the moment when other ghost plants grow so far as to cover it, the hill the ridge the coast flooding into a single lake the shadows

So I could limit my description to the dark areas that expand and shrink depending on the time of day with a rotary movement rendered streaky and uneven by the different levels and inclinations of the terrain, now swallowing up and now revealing vines, seedbeds, yellow fields of marigolds, black gardens of magnolias, red quarries of stone, markets, everywhere the shade has its rendezvous and its itineraries, here it is entitled to reign over entire valleys, there it can do no more than gather scraps of itself hidden away behind a watering can or a wheelbarrow, every place can be defined according to a scale ranging from those places never reached by the sun to those exposed to its light from dawn to dusk

Let us call those areas the sun doesn't reach "opaque", while those it does we can call "sunny," or "sunshiny". Since the world I am describing is a sort of concave amphitheatre on the south side and since it does not include the convex face of the amphitheatre, presumably looking north, it thus turns out that the opaque is extremely rare and the sunny more widespread

or choosing to resort to a metaphor taken from animal life, we are in a world that stretches and twists like a lizard so as to offer the largest possible surface area to the sun, opening up the fan of its suction-cup feet on a wall that's growing warm, its tail retreating with threadlike jerks from the imperceptible advance of the shade, eager to have the sunny coincide with the existence of the world

eager to have the sunny coincide with the struggle for existence and that at once and with maximum profit, levelling out the declivities in the geometrical empire of the carnations whose square legions push forward into the sunshine in serried ranks, or righting the vertical walls of the apartment blocks chequered with windows that vie for the best exposure and view

Only at the bottom of streams bristling with reeds that rustle like paper, or in sharply twisting valleys, or behind the protruding tops of the hills, and further back in the succession of spurs along the mountain chain parallel to the coast, is there that darkening of the green, that outcropping of rocks from the rain-washed earth, that nearness of a cold that rises from beneath the ground, that remoteness not only from the invisible sea but also from the fierce blue of the overarching sky, that sense of a mysterious border separating this from the open and alien world, which is the sense of having entered into the opaque reverse side of the world

so that I could define the opaque as a declaration that the world I am describing does have a reverse side, the possibility that I might find myself otherwise placed and orientated, in a different relationship with the trajectory of the sun and the dimensions of infinite space, a sign that the world presupposes a rest of the world, beyond the barrier of the mountains ranged behind my back, a world that extends into the opaque with towns and cities and highlands and watercourses and marshes, with

mountain chains that conceal fog-bound pla-
teaus, I sense this reverse side of the world
hidden beyond the deep thickness of earth and
rock, and immediately it becomes the vertigo
roaring in my ears and thrusting me towards
the elsewhere

So now this reconstruction of the world accomplished in the absence of the world ought
to start over again supposing me flattened in my
lizard-like immobility on the rugged sunshiny
slope but at the same time supposing me thrust
vertiginously towards the elsewhere, and here
I would open a parenthesis to distinguish one
elsewhere as absolute sunniness opening on a
sea furrowed by distant ferryboats and one elsewhere as absolute opaqueness opening up before
whoever looks out beyond a furthest mountain
ridge

or perhaps the elsewheres converge, the ship
I see leaving the shore and disappearing in the
sun's glare will drop anchor in opaque ports,
will see grey banks of wharves looming from
morning fog, lights still lit on the docks,

———

and the hunter who follows the mule track up into the moorlands enters the wood, climbs the ridge of the mountain, skirts a sheltered hollow, sends stones rolling into the bushes hoping to flush out a flock of partridges, runs down across the meadows, climbs up a rocky crag, searches out the trail of migratory birds, searches out the summit beyond which the view of a boundless land opens up before his eyes, the watershed of all watersheds, the roof of the world, whence to lean out and gaze far away beyond the great wing of shadow, so far as to make out a golden-gated Thule, a Helsinki with its white piazza, sunny city on a bay of ice

And even if we consider the observer immobile as at the beginning, his situation with regard to the opaque and the sunny will still be a matter for debate, since that self of mine turned to face the sunny area becomes the opaque side it sees of every bridge tree roof, while the wall or slope to which I turn my back is in full sunshine, the wall blooming with bougainvillea, the slope with its tufts of spurge, the hedge of Turkish figs, the trellis of capers

———

but that's not what matters because granted I am still looking towards the mouth of whatever valley I'm in with my back turned to the tumbling shadowy stream, there is nothing to guarantee that I am about to advance further and further into the open rather than going backward into the depths of the valley, so that the correct thing to say is that the self turned towards the sunny side is nevertheless a self withdrawing into the opaque

And if departing from that initial position I consider the successive phases of that same self of mine, every step forward could just as well be a retreat, the line I trace is ever more cloaked in the opaque, and it is pointless trying to remember just where I entered the shadow, I was already there at the beginning, it is pointless searching in the depths of the opaque for an escape from the opaque, I now know that the only world that exists is the opaque the sunny being nothing more than its reverse side, the sunny that opaquely struggles to multiply itself while doing nothing more than to multiply the reverse of its own reverse

From the opaque, from the depths of the opaque I write, reconstructing the map of a sunniness that is only an unverifiable postulate for the computations of the memory, the geometrical location of the ego, of a self which the self needs to know that it is itself, the ego whose only function is that the world may continually receive news of the existence of the world, a contrivance at the service of the world for knowing if it exists.